D1099973

Kenya

Front cover: White-bearded wildebeest

Right: The Maasai giraffe, identifiable by its ragged spot pattern

TOP 10 ATTRACTIONS

The Maasai Mara • Where great herds of animals roam the plains; also home to the Maasai tribe *(page 71)*

The Amboseli • With its impressive Mount Kilimanjaro backdrop, few places are as spectacular for elephant spotting *(page 75)*

The Great Rift Valley • Its lakes are famed for their fabulous birdlife *(page 57)*

Kenya's coast • Characterised by gorgeous white sands and palm trees *(page 80)*

Samburu National Reserve • See beautiful landscapes and species found only in the north of the country *(page 54)*

The Tsavo • Divided into East and West, it's the largest national park in Kenya *(page 76)*

Nairobi • The country's bustling capital is the first stop for most visitors *(page 43)*

Mombasa • This historic crossroads of Africa and Asia is Kenya's oldest city *(page 80)*

Lamu • Visting the island is like stepping back in time *(page 87)*

Mount Kenya • Part of the Central Highlands, this extinct volcano offers spectacular views *(page 53)*

CONTENTS

64

69

37

102

73

50

INTRODUCTION

Travel through Kenya and you will see all of Africa in one country. If you drive cross-country, you will be surprised how quickly the landscape changes: dropping down from fertile highlands into semi-arid plains, emerging from a lush mountain forest to sweep through a vast plateau, climbing up a steep escarpment from the deep trench of the Rift Valley, or turning off coconut palm-lined tarmac on to a dusty dirt track.

Kenya is a country of contradictions, where snow lies on the equator, and semi-deserts flood in the long rains. Blue lakes turn pink when blanketed with a million flamingos; the icy top of Mount Kilimanjaro shimmers over Amboseli's arid plains. In contrast to the rich diversity of the south-west – home to 85 percent of the population – the vast northern and eastern regions, nearly two-thirds of the country, are wilderness.

The language

The Swahili language, which is essentially Bantu, with an infusion of Arabic, Asian and European words, has become the *lingua franca* for about 60 million people in eastern Africa.

The country has long been a favourite safari destination. Big-game hunting expeditions, however, are a thing of the past, and the only shooting allowed today is with a camera. But even with the rigours of the bush eased by organised game drives and comfortable safari vehicles, little matches the thrill of seeing your first herd of elephants or pride of lions in the wild.

If, on the other hand, you want nothing more demanding from your holiday than to lie under a palm tree, Kenya's coastline offers long stretches of unspoiled beach and fabulous coral reefs, interspersed with swish resorts.

Young man from Nairobi

The acacia tree is a striking feature of the savannah

Cultural Diversity

With over 40 tribes and tribal languages, Kenya's national heritage is a patchwork quilt of history and customs, sewn together by the colonial threads of the late 19th and early 20th centuries. Tribal differences are Kenya's greatest cultural asset, and one of its most formidable social and political challenges. Surprisingly, perhaps, the tribes are formations that rarely go back more than a couple of hundred years and were sustained as elements of colonial administration at a time when they were progressively merging and dissolving.

The divisions that Kenyans make in defining their origins are mainly linguistic: Bantu-, Nilotic-, Nilo-Hamitic- and Hamitic-speaking peoples. The Kikuyu of the central highlands, part of the Bantu-speaking majority, are the largest tribe, comprising nearly half of the population; they enjoy considerable prestige and influence despite efforts to lessen their dominance. They are followed by the Luo, from the shores of Lake Victoria, and the Luhya of the western farmlands who make up another 29 percent; followed by the Kalenjin and the Kamba.

Kenya's most famous tribe is the Maasai, a group of tall, pastoral nomads who resist the encroachments of modern civilisation. They guard their cattle herds with spears and wear their traditional red cloaks and bright beaded jewellery.

Asians, Arabs and Europeans form a small but vital minority. The Indo-Pakistani communities who emigrated here during colonial times retain control over much of the country's retail businesses. Arab residents go back much further to the coastal settlements founded in the Middle Ages. Kiswahili is the lingua franca that ties them all together, though English is also an official language.

The land once ruled by the Europeans has been largely returned to African hands. But the colonial legacy is marked by the prevalence of the English language, customs and, for want of a better word, cuisine. Vehicles drive on the left, and the structure of government and public services all show the abiding influence of British models.

With an estimated 34 million people, half of whom are under the age of 15, Kenya has one of the highest rates of population growth in the world. Yet only about one quarter of the land is arable. With this equation, poverty threatens to become more visible and more widespread. Yet, despite this, Kenya's social problems are not glaringly apparent.

Fruit seller on Mombasa beach

What will strike you instead is the friendliness and easy-going nature of the people. Outside the larger cities there is a genuine interest in visitors and delight in casual chat. All along the road children wave; even the fearsome Maasai will often raise a hand in greeting.

Ups and Downs

Kenya is seen as an oasis of calm and stability on a continent that has known little but turmoil in the decades since decolonisation. This image has been a great advantage in attracting the tourist trade; indeed, tourism has become one of the mainstays of the economy, with tea, coffee and horticulture, being the major foreign income earners. But recently, cracks have appeared in this veneer.

Much of the country's stability has been maintained through iron-handed rule. The elections of December 1992 *(see page 20)* provoked violent ethnic clashes in the provinces,

Kilimanjaro

Except for the beginnings of its northern foothills, Kilimanjaro is entirely inside Tanzania, but the awe-inspiring view of it from Amboseli makes it an undeniable part of Kenya's landscape. At 5,895m (19,342ft), this vast, extinct volcano is Africa's highest mountain. It has three great peaks: the highest is the snow-covered table known as Kibo, called Uhuru (freedom) since Tanzania gained independence; the western peak, Shira, is 4,005m (13,140ft); the eastern peak is Mawenzi, 5,150m (16,897ft) high, but tougher to climb than Kibo. Legend has it that the son of King Solomon and the Queen of Sheba, King Menelik of Abyssinia, also made it to the top. In heroic battles he conquered all of East Africa and then, as death approached, he climbed Kibo. He disappeared into the crater with his slaves, who carried his treasures, including Solomon's ring. Find that ring and you'll inherit Solomon's wisdom and Menelik's courage.

and fears of political unrest kept many tourists away. These fears were unfounded, as Kenyans accepted the election results peaceably and got on with their daily affairs, preferring to restore equilibrium than to incite confrontation. The new opposition parties, however, continue to clamour for political change. Much anticipated multi-party elections were held in December 2002, with a landslide victory for Mwai Kibaki heading the National Rainbow Coalition (NARC), giving Kenya a new ruling party for the first time since independence.

Lioness and cub share a quiet moment together

More alarming threats come from outside Kenya's borders. The conflicts in neighbouring Somalia, Ethiopia, Uganda and the Sudan have spilled into the northern region, in the form of occasional bandit attacks and an influx of refugees. Outbreaks of poaching, though largely eliminated, sometimes flare up in the game parks. While these occurrences seldom endanger the casual tourist, always follow the advice of the authorities when travelling in remote regions, and respect any no-go areas. That said, when you go to Kenya, be prepared for an exciting sensory experience. You will have a trip here as you have never had before, and you'll also come back keener, more alive and more demanding of your usual surroundings.

A BRIEF HISTORY

East Africa has been called the 'cradle of mankind', and prehistoric man may well have taken his first footsteps across the savannah lands of Kenya. In 1972 a fossil skull was found at Koobi Fora on the shores of Lake Turkana; between two and three million years old, it is the oldest ancestor of modern man found to date. It now sits in the Nairobi Museum, tagged with the simple moniker 'No. 1470'.

Some theories hold that the climate and topography of East Africa provided the right environment for human evolution and that, over hundreds of thousands of years, these early ancestors migrated from this region to populate other continents. Whatever the case, some of the earliest remains of Stone Age man have been found in Kenya at sites on Rusinga Island, Hyrax Hill, Kariandusi and Olorgesailie.

Kenya's earliest societies were hunter-gatherers. Cattle-herding and agriculture emerged only c.1000BC. In fact, Kenya seems to have remained largely at a Stone Age level until c.AD1000, when signs of iron-smelting appeared, brought by Bantu-speaking tribes from the west and south. The gradual change from a hunting-and-gathering society to one of agriculture led to rapid increases in population in the fertile areas of the highlands and the grazing plateaux of the southwest.

Settlement of the Coast

Arabs landed on the Kenya coast in the 7th century AD, looking to develop trade between East Africa and the Far East. Later, the rise of Islam in the Middle East caused a wave of migration to the coastal strip – a pattern that continued into the 12th century. The intermingling of these settlers from the Persian Gulf with the Bantu population gave rise to the mixed Bantu-Arabic language of Kiswahili. The Swahilis produced

Kenya's first written language, in Arabic characters. Though the Islamic influence was pervasive, Swahili culture was also affected by interaction with Asia and the Far East.

Over the next 300 years, the Swahili trading centres, scattered along the coastline, developed into powerful city-states, notably Mombasa, Malindi and Lamu. They produced iron and ceramics and traded with ships from Persia, India and the Far East, exchanging animal skins, ivory, tortoiseshell, gums and spices for sugar, grain and cloth. In 1498 Vasco da Gama, searching for a sea route to India, landed in Malindi. The Portuguese soon returned to plunder the rich coastal cities. While Mombasa fiercely resisted the encroachment, the Portuguese formed a trading alliance with its rival state, Malindi. Mombasa was attacked three times in the 16th century before being surrendered to the Portuguese in 1592.

From their new military garrison at Fort Jesus the Portuguese reigned for the next century, but their hold was weakened by repeated native attacks and threats to their position elsewhere in the Indian Ocean and the Gulf. In 1660 the Sultan of Oman supported a major revolt on Pate Island, north of Lamu. The Portuguese occupants were finally driven out of Mombasa in 1698.

Aided by British naval technology, the Omanis sup-

Fort Jesus, Mombasa

pressed the Swahili rebellions and became the new foreign over-
lords on the coast. Ruling from Zanzibar, they cultivated the
ivory trade with the interior; then, in the 1830s, a new trade,
slavery, proved more lucrative. By 1854 it had crossed over
Kenya's borders into Uganda. Slavery was officially forbidden
in 1873, but it took 20 years for the illegal trade to cease.

The Interior in the Late 19th Century

Prior to British colonisation, Kenya's interior was populated
by groups that took a long time to achieve tribal unity.
Throughout this period there was a constant migration and
merging of peoples now identified as Bantu-, Nilotic-, Nilo-
Hamitic- or Hamitic-speaking. Tribal identity developed slowly, following the change from a pastoral to an agricultural way
of life, and the ensuing fight for land ownership among tribes.

The Maa speakers, namely the Maasai and Samburu, were
the last tribal group to arrive in Kenya. Gradually moving
southward, within a few generations these obscure nomads had
expanded along the plains and throughout the Rift Valley, to
eventually become a strong force from Lake Turkana to Mount
Kilimanjaro. Differences between Maasai groups erupted in the
Maasai Civil Wars in the last half of the 19th century.

Political organisation varied greatly among these ethnic
groups. The Bantus of northwestern Kenya had a certain cen-
tralised organisation, with a council of elders advising a clan
leader paid for his services in meat, grain or beer. But the
eastern Bantu people – most prominently the Kikuyu – were
organised in peer groups known as age-sets, each serving a
military, polic or judicial function in ruling the tribal lands.
Solidarity came through kinship and territorial allegiance,
rather than loyalty to a central council of chief.

Arab caravans from Mombasa ventured into the interior
on ivory safaris, trading mainly with the Kamba tribe. The
quality of the ivory from Kenya's elephants was considered

superior to that of their Indian cousins and sold better in the Orient. The caravans opened up routes from Mombasa to Kilimanjaro, across the Rift Valley to Lake Victoria and even as far north as Lake Turkana. The Arabs, however, were never able to gain a hold on the interior itself.

Missionaries and adventurers from Britain and Germany had moved up-country as early as 1846, laying the groundwork for later colonisation. Two of them, Johann Ludwig Krapf and Johann Rebmann, located Mounts Kenya and Kilimanjaro; another – John Hanning Speke – 'discovered' Lake Victoria in 1858, whilst Joseph Thompson explored Maasai territory in 1883. When the Europeans carved up the continent, Kenya, Uganda and Zanzibar went to the British, and Tanganyika (Tanzania) to the Germans. Each monarch got a snow-capped peak: Mount Kenya for Queen Victoria and Mount Kilimanjaro for Kaiser Wilhelm.

British cruisers capturing a Kenyan island in 1875

Under the Union Jack

The British colonised Kenya almost as an afterthought. They were, in fact, far more interested in their prospects in Zanzibar and Uganda. For several years, they left Kenya to the administration of the Imperial British East Africa Company (est. 1888), which imposed taxes, built trading posts and pursued the ivory trade in the interior. Inept management of the territory forced the British government to take over the operation of what it called the 'East Africa Protectorate' seven years later.

A means of transport was needed between the coast and the source of the River Nile to reduce costs and develop plantation agriculture. In 1896 construction began on a railway line to connect Mombasa with Port Florence, today's Kisumu, which was later extended into Uganda. To pay for the high cost of the project, the government publicised the previously remote highlands as a great farming and settlement region. Immigrants from Britain, Europe and South Africa flooded in.

Early 20th-century satire of the Great White Hunter

Lord Delamere, a pioneer agriculturalist, became champion of the white settlers. In 1903 he was given a grant of 40,000ha (98,840 acres) of rich farmland in the central highlands, north of Nairobi. Other settlers also appropriated huge landed estates for themselves, and introduced coffee, tea and pineapples. Cereals and other European crops also thrived, and this fertile region soon became known as the 'White Highlands'.

Within a few years, half of the prime farmland was controlled by the settlers. The Kikuyu were driven out and resettled on native reserves, where the growing population faced grave land shortages. Many had no choice but to work for the settlers as farm labourers and domestic servants. Colonial authorities imposed control by appointing tribal chiefs to collect hut taxes. A new class structure developed, as young Africans competed for wealth and privileges conferred by these chieftainships. One of the most hated laws required Africans to register and carry ID cards.

Apart from Swahili towns on the coast, Kenya's urban areas were all European in origin. Africans could work but not live there, except as 'sojourners' in shanty towns on the outskirts. Indians as well as Africans were denied farming rights in the White Highlands. In 1907 the capital of the protectorate was shifted from Mombasa to Nairobi, but it was not until 1920 that the region became known as the Crown Colony of Kenya, a name derived from the country's highest peak.

African Ascendency

World War I had a profound effect on the 200,000 African soliders who were conscripted into the British army. Living and fighting side by side in the campaign for Tanganyika, Kenyans learned military tactics and witnessed at first hand the white man's real strengths and weaknesses. At the end of the war, the Soldier Resettlement Scheme rewarded the white servicemen with new land rights, while Kenyans returned to impoverished living conditions. This caused great bitterness, and political activist groups sprang up, made up chiefly of Kikuyu ex-soldiers.

The strongest group was the East African Association, led by a government clerk named Harry Thuku. At the peak of the protests in 1921, Thuku was arrested and imprisoned for 11 years. Other militant groups, such as the Kikuyu Central Association (KCA), carried on the nationalist movement. It was known as Uhuru: the call for independence.

In the 1920s and 1930s, settlers in the White Highlands enjoyed an unprecedented heyday of good fortune. Meanwhile, the government tried to diffuse the clamour for independence by courting the more moderate among the African leaders. In 1944 Eliud Mathu was made the first African member of Kenya's Legislative Council. Moreover, he was also permitted to form an advisory group.

Just two years later, Jomo Kenyatta, one of the movement's first leaders, returned to Nairobi after 16 years of study and political activism in England. He took over Mathu's advisory group, renamed it the Kenya African Union, and set about transforming the small educated elite into a mass political movement open to all workers and war veterans.

However, differences grew between Kenyatta's radicals – who sought independence through revolutionary methods –

Out of Africa

A casualty of the early 20th century was the first Baroness (Karen) Blixen, whose hunter husband, Bror, went off with another woman and left her to go bankrupt on a suburban Nairobi coffee farm under the Ngong Hills. Her memoir, *Out of Africa* – remarkable for its stylish insight on the country and people – was eloquent on the since exaggerated and romanticised high life of Kenya in the 1920s and 1930s. She entertained Edward, Prince of Wales, and had her own romantic interlude with a raffish member of the club, the Hon. Denys Finch Hatton. But the overall impression was that of a slightly desperate gaiety, rather like that of pre-Revolutionary Russia in *The Cherry Orchard*. The peasant revolution, in the form of the Kikuyu independence movement, was close at hand.

and the moderates surrounding Eliud Mathu, who wanted a reformist approach. The moderates especially resented Kikuyu domination of the KAU, and Kenyatta agreed that multi-tribal leadership was essential to national independence, a problem that plagued him after independence was achieved.

The Mau Mau

An underground movement arose when Kikuyus took secret oaths against the British government, sparking guerilla attacks against settlers in the White Highlands. The Mau Mau rebellion is believed to have been named after a Kikuyu warning that

Karen Blixen's home and the setting for *Out of Africa*

the enemy was coming. A state of emergency was declared in 1952, and though the KAU did not participate in the attacks, Kenyatta and other leaders were jailed.

The fighting was fierce. Thousands of Kikuyus, Embus and Merus were resettled in guarded areas. In 1956, British troops drove the Mau Mau bands into the Mount Kenya and Aberdare forests, where they were killed or captured. The casualties of the rebellion numbered over 11,000 Mau Mau, 2,000 African civilians, 50 British troops and 95 European settlers.

The armed rebellion was broken, but colonial authority was at an end. In 1960 the White Highlands, covering 800,000ha (1,976,840 acres), were opened up to black ownership.

However, Kenya's tribal conflicts remained unresolved, as the Kikuyu-dominated Kenya African National Union (KANU) competed for power with the Kenya African Democratic Union (KADU) of the minority tribes. Jomo Kenyatta returned from exile to lead KANU in 1961. Independence was finally achieved on 12 December 1963, and, when a republic was proclaimed the next year, Kenyatta was named president.

Independence

Kenyatta began his presidency under the banner of Harambee: 'pulling together'. His skill in transferring power to African hands, while courting the aid and support of the former colonial rulers, earned him the title of respect, Mzee, or 'Honourable Old Man', while Kenya emerged as a model of democracy and progress among African countries.

After the election the KADU opposition was dissolved, and Kenya became a one-party state. There was growing corruption and internal unrest, but political dissent was squashed by persecution and the fear generated by the assassination of Tom Mboya, a Luo politician tipped to become the next president. Kikuyu dominance grew, and when Kenyatta died suddenly in August 1978, he did so as one of the world's richest men.

Daniel arap Moi, a member of the minority Kalenjin tribe, was chosen to succeed Kenyatta in order to combat tribal rivalry between the Kikuyu and the Luo. His initial efforts to wipe out tribalism and corruption were well received but short-lived. The next decade was marred by an attempted military coup in August 1982, accusations of internal plots against the government, student unrest and human-rights violations.

Kenya had long enjoyed influxes of foreign aide, but during the early 1990s Western donors, alarmed at reports of widespread corruption and political repression, suspended further aid until the Moi government demonstrated progress on human rights and political reform. As a result, in late December 1992, Kenya held its first multi-party elections since independence. The opposition parties that emerged were unable to form a united block to unseat Moi, who was re-elected amid accusations of vote-rigging and ethnic clashes in the provinces.

However, the foundation had been laid for change, as Kenyans continued to strive for stability, growth and prosperity. Elections were held in 1997, but again the opposition parties were not strong enough to defeat KANU. In the late 1990s the IMF imposed a three-year freeze on funds – a block that finally ended in July 2000. A new poverty reduction and growth facility was agreed upon by the government and the IMF, but this failed again on the grounds of the government not meeting its commitments on governance.

In 2001 Moi appointed Raila Odinga and three members of the National Development Party (NDP) and set the stage for the first coalition government in Kenya's post-independent

Commemorating Jomo Kenyatta in Nairobi

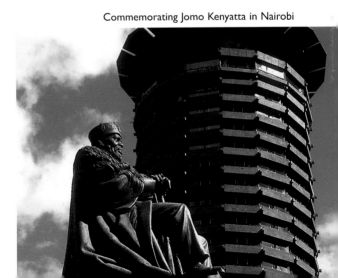

history. KANU merged with the NDP in early 2002, with Moi finally picking Uhuru Kenyatta to succeed him. The Rainbow Alliance was then formed, comprising former NDP members in KANU and other leading KANU members. This Rainbow Alliance formally broke away from KANU and transformed itself into the Liberal Democratic Party (LDP) and merged with Ford-People to form the National Rainbow Coalition (NARC). In the December 2002 Presidential elections, Mwai Kibaki won a landslide victory, as did NARC, bringing into power a new ruling party for the first time since independence in 1963.

In November 2002 Islamic terrorists attacked the Paradise Hotel near Mombasa with a suicide bomb, killing 13 people, illustrating the weakness of Kenya's security. In 2003 there were further security warnings when commercial flights from the UK were suspended for six weeks. This did not bode well for Kenya's tourism industry, but it served as a wake-up call, prompting major players in the industry to promote Kenya tourism overseas. The country is now reaping the benefits with major bookings in hotels and lodges around the country.

Kenya's political system is currently in a state of uncertainty. It was announced on 30 December 2007 that Mwai Kibaki's Party of National Unity had narrowly defeated Raila Odinga's Orange Democratic Movement in the Presidential elections. The disputed results unleashed a wave of unrest across Kenya, causing hundreds of deaths and the feared displacement of thousands more. In early 2008, it was hoped that both sides would agree to work together to resolve the political crisis.

Beads are a Maasai hallmark

Historical Landmarks

1.8 million BC Ancestral hominids living on the shores of Lake Turkana.

AD500,000 Cushitic, Nilotic and Bantu peoples move into Kenya.

c.900 Arrival of Islam, marking the beginning of the coast's golden age.

14th century Swahili community emerges.

1498 Vasco da Gama arrives in Malindi.

1824 Kenya claimed as a British Protectorate.

1849 First European sighting of Mount Kenya by Austrian Johan Krapf.

1886 Kenya and Uganda are assigned to the British.

1914–18 World War I.

1921 Harry Thuku arrested. Protesting Kenyans massacred in Nairobi.

1939–45 World War II.

1944 Start of Mau Mau rebellion.

1952 Simmering Kenyan nationalism. State of emergency called following attacks against white settlers. Kenyatta and other leaders are imprisoned.

1959 Kenyatta released and put under house arrest.

1963 Kenya gains independence; Kenyatta is first elected president.

1964 Kenya declared a republic.

1978 Daniel Toroitich arap Moi becomes president on death of Kenyatta.

1982 Attempted coup by rebels in the Kenyan Air Force is put down.

1992 First multi-party elections for 26 years are held. Moi is re-elected.

1993 Economic crisis: Kenyan shilling devalued by around 50 percent.

1997 Moi is re-elected president.

1998 Heavy rains caused by El Niño wreak devastation. Islamic terrorists plant a car bomb near US Embassy in Nairobi, killing over 200 people.

2002 13 people killed by a terrorist attack in Mombasa. Mwai Kibaki of the National Rainbow Coalition wins the presidential elections.

2003 Government introduces free primary education.

2004 Referendum on new constitution.

2005 74 people killed in raids on a village in northeast Kenya. Kenyan electorate resoundingly rejects new draft constitution in a referendum.

2006 Widespread flooding renders thousands homeless.

2007 Riots break out as Kibaki's election victory is called into question.

WHERE TO GO

Life in the Kenyan capital, Nairobi, can claim to be fairly advanced, but from there on, a safari in Kenya backtracks in time, following the millennia down to the origins of man around Lake Turkana. The remains of times long past are evident across the country. Immediately north of Nairobi massive volcanoes that appeared after ancient geological upheavals have fallen in to form the Great Rift Valley. The sentinel Mount Kenya stands over the agricultural heartland of the country. The Age of the Mammals is evident all over Kenya, but exemplified in more than 40 national parks and game reserves, where the animals and pristine landscapes are entirely conserved.

National Parks and Game Reserves

Indeed, Kenya's monuments are not cathedrals or palaces but great wildlife that roams the length and breadth of the country. Animals and birds are accorded a privileged position and are protected against the wanton hunting and poaching that have nearly decimated many species. In 1989 Dr Richard Leakey, anthropologist and conservationist, became head of the Kenya Wildlife Service (KWS). His efforts to eliminate poaching and improve conditions and safety within the parks have been largely successful, enabling visitors to enjoy 50 conservation areas comprising 7 percent of the country's total land area.

Protecting Kenya's wildlife is no small task. The parks are under intense pressure both from commercial developers and the growing population. Soil, trees and other vegetation that make up the eco-system must also be conserved for the animals to survive. Most parks in Kenya are not fenced, allowing game to migrate freely back and forth through transitional

Migrating wildebeest crossing the Mara River

zones, but this natural order is becoming increasingly threatened as man and beast compete for the land and its resources.

KWS has begun a number of community wildlife programmes, whereby a portion of the gate takings at the parks is set aside for development projects in the adjacent areas, thereby enabling the local communities to see a direct benefit from wildlife conservation.

Kenya's national parks do not stop at the water's edge. A coral reef runs along nearly the entire length of the coast, and several marine national parks and reserves have been established to preserve this fascinating underwater ecosystem of live corals, tropical fish and marine animals.

Safaris – a Swahili word meaning 'journey' – are organised into the bush in four-wheel-drive vehicles and minibuses with pop-up roofs that allow wildlife viewing and photography at close quarters. Just after sunrise and late afternoon are the best times for a game drive, before and after the animals settle down to rest in the heat of the day.

Ecotourism

This is a growing market in Kenya: an increasing number of ranches and local communities are offering safari holidays that preserve and foster both the wildlife and the culture in their area. To raise funds for conservation and social projects, they build small lodges using local materials, and staff them with trained personnel from the area. The fees are used for local projects – schools, dispensaries, water supply – which also provide employment.

Many of these community-run eco-lodges are to be found in the Laikipia/Samburu region, including Il Ngwesi, Tassia, Borana and the Lewa Wildlife Conservancy. Namunyak is slightly further north in the Mathews Range, and Shompole overlooks Lake Magadi at the southern end of the Great Rift Valley. These lodges are often in stunning locations, with a wide scope for exploring, game drives, walks and birdwatching.

Close encounter

Game spotting is definitely an acquired skill, and the services of a driver or guide are invaluable; he can take you to the places most likely to shelter the more elusive animals, and provide useful information and folklore about the animals' habits. Keep on the lookout: animals have a natural camouflage, and without an experienced pair of eyes you may never notice that cheetah sinking slowly into the tall grass.

You will have many opportunities for photographing, filming and simply viewing with binoculars, but remember that safari is all luck. Keep in mind, as you read or hear about what species you can expect to see at this or that park, that they're not always to be found in the same place. Animals migrate, weather conditions change and availability of food and water varies daily. During dry periods they tend to congregate around waterholes; after a rainy spell the vegetation is higher and denser, making the animals much harder to see. It's better to relax and enjoy whatever the luck of the safari brings your way.

THE BIG FIVE

The idea of a 'Big Five' dates from the days when white hunters led safaris, the principal objective of which was to shoot wild beasts for trophies. Inevitably, some creatures were regarded as more desirable targets than others, reflecting the skill it took to track them, the risk involved in confronting them and the quality of the trophy retrieved from a successful kill. In time, five mammals that qualified on all counts were recognised as the ultimate objectives of a hunting safari: the buffalo, elephant, leopard, lion and rhinoceros. Today, hunting is outlawed in Kenya but the Big Five still have their cachet.

Buffalo
The African buffalo is traditionally known as the meanest beast in the bush, prone to launch a charge at the drop of a

Famously fearsome buffalo

hat. As grazers, buffalos are generally found in grassland, where they do most of their feeding and moving around in the evening, night and early morning. Buffalos, which weigh up to 800kg (1,750lb), must drink daily, so are never found more than 15km (9 miles) from water. Like domestic cattle, they probably sleep for no more than an hour a day.

Amboseli elephant

Buffalos live in herds of relatively stable size. They may number up to 2,000, but large herds tend to fragment during the dry season and regroup in the wet. This spreads the grazing load when grass is in short supply. Bachelor groups of 10 to 15 are common, and consist either of old, retired bulls who no longer bother to keep competing for females, or younger bulls nearing their prime. Solitary old males or small bull groups are the animals most likely to charge intruders.

Elephant

Although the lion has long been regarded as the king of beasts, when you see animals working out their own hierarchy in nature, you are likely to conclude that the supreme monarch is the elephant. An adult male, 3m (10ft) tall, often weighs over 5,400kg (11,905lb) and each tusk may weigh up to 90kg (198lb). The female, just under 3m, weighs a mere 3,500kg (7,700lb). But it is the females who do all the work, are the leaders of herds and group their own baby and adolescent offspring and that of their daughters. Male elephants are chased away from the herd as soon as they are old enough to fend for themselves (12 to 14 years) and join up with other males.

Enormously affectionate, female elephants also do all the fighting to protect their young from lions and hyenas. The males turn up only when one of the females goes into heat. Pregnancy lasts up to 22 months, the longest of any mammal. Living till a grand old age of 50 to 60 years, elephants are known to bury their own dead and indeed other dead animals, even dead human beings they have killed: but, contrary to legend, they do not have mass burial grounds.

Leopard

Leopards are always described as elusive, and you will indeed be lucky to see one unless you happen to be in one of those game lodges that lure leopards to floodlit platforms with bait. Leopards keep to the cover of trees or dense undergrowth and their solitary, stealthy habits enable them to survive the attention of poachers much better than lions and cheetahs.

Magnificent female leopard

Females seem to roam at will, while male leopards are definitely territorial, staking out their home range by spraying urine along the boundaries and fighting off other males who might trespass. The big feline's usual roar sounds like wood sawing, but during mating it turns into a snarling and caterwauling reminiscent of alley cats, only around ten times louder. Unlike cheetahs, the females make very affectionate mothers and continue to meet up with their offspring, even after they've grown up and left home.

Leopards, like cats, are nocturnal beasts, spending the day resting in the shade, either under an overhanging hillside rock or up a tree, anywhere, in fact, where they can survey the surrounding countryside. Weighing between 35 and 55kg (75 and 120lb) on average, they are powerful and versatile hunters, prepared to kill anything from small birds to animals as much as three times their size. Leopards can carry up to 45kg (100lb) of uneaten meat into the higher branches of a tree, out of the reach of scavengers. They particularly enjoy eating other carnivores such as foxes, jackals and serval cats, among others. This accounts for their notorious partiality for domestic dogs on occasions when they have wandered into town.

Lion

The lion is, arguably, the king of the jungle, though nobody would dispute that this is the most feared of African predators. Lions are ferocious hunters, but in the daylight hours when you will see them, they are more likely to seem docile, lazy, imperturbable and even downright friendly. Unless, of course, they were unable to find a meal during the night, in which case their hunger might rouse them into action.

Lion prides, made up of several small families spread over a wide area, are more loosely knit groups than elephant herds. Lions roam over a territory that covers perhaps as much as 50sq km (some 20sq miles) in groups of threes and fours, usually lionesses with their cubs, while male lions tend to roam together, keeping separate from the females until mealtime.

With an arrogance that would enrage the mildest feminist, the male leaves almost all the hunting to the female and just waits for the kill, at which point he finally throws his weight around (240kg/528lb compared with the female's 150kg/

330lb), moves in, fights off the lioness and her cubs and takes... the lion's share. In the male's defence, we can only say that his presence as a sentinel does keep the pride area safe for the lioness and her cubs.

The lion's favourite prey is zebra and buffalo. Both are big enough to provide a hearty meal for the whole family, but also strong enough, especially buffalo, to require group effort for a kill. Most antelopes can be knocked off single-handedly.

Lions are extremely sensuous beasts. They like to lick, groom and rub up against each other, often as an act of group solidarity before the hunt or just out of good fellowship during the after-dinner siesta. Male lions are especially vain about grooming their opulent mane, their chief sexual selling-point. The roar, heard most often before dawn or early evening, is a crescendo of deep rolling grunts quite unlike that fabricated MGM groan.

Maasai Mara lion lazing in the afternoon

Rhinoceros

The number of rhinos in Kenya have dwindled from 8,000 in the 1960s to fewer than 1,000. Although they may move around in groups of two and three, they tend to live alone. There is nothing more desolate than the screaming groan of a solitary rhino disturbed by another at his waterhole. However, there is one creature that can approach the rhino with impunity: the little oxpecker (or tick bird), which perches on the rhino's back. In exchange for the rhino's ticks and flies, the oxpecker provides a loudly chattering alarm system to warn the sleeping rhino of any approaching danger.

Black or white

The two African species, 'black' and 'white' rhinos, are in fact both grey. 'White' is a corruption of the Afrikaans word for 'wide', referring to its mouth.

Mother rhinos are ferocious defenders of their young. A concerted attack by three male lions on a rhino calf can result in one of the lions being killed and the other two slinking away. The rhino can move his 2,000+kg (4,400lb) bulk up to 55kph (35mph), at least as fast as a lion, with an amazing ability to wheel suddenly to face an attack from the rear.

There's nothing remotely delicate about rhinos, not even their love-making, which is accompanied by ferocious snorting and jousting resistance from the female before she submits. Unlike the few seconds expended by most animals, copulation between rhinos lasts more than 30 minutes, and this is thought to account for the mythic properties attributed to that horn.

OTHER PREDATORS

The predators in the 'Big Five' are not the only animals to live by hunting and killing; others include cheetahs, smaller cats, dogs, jackals, foxes, mongooses, genets and civets.

Cheetah

Cheetahs are not very gregarious, often hunting alone and so unable to protect their kill when attacked by scavenging lions, hyenas or even vultures. A mother will dutifully rear her cubs and then part quite abruptly from them. They never acknowledge each other again. Male cheetahs fend for themselves, occasionally hunting with a couple of males, and meeting up with females exclusively for mating – and then only after a fierce fight.

Proud cheetah

The mother's training of her cubs for hunting is a careful affair, as would befit the fastest mammal on earth: an amazing 112kph (70mph). At first, the mother cheetah makes the kill herself, usually by biting through the prey's windpipe. The cub picks up the dead prey by the throat and 'strangles' it again. Gradually, the mother lets the growing cub have first go at catching the prey, and only if he botches it will she intervene, so as not to risk totally losing the meal.

Alternatively, the mother makes the first thrust and then leaves the weakened prey for the cub to finish off. When he reaches 14 months, the cub is considered ready to do the job alone. You have a fair chance of seeing a cheetah hunt, as it is the only big cat to do so by day.

Spot the difference

A cheetah's body markings are round spots with pronounced black 'tear-marks' on the face, whereas the leopard's spots are like groups of five fingerprints and its face is spotted rather than 'tear-marked'.

Hyena

With their oversized heads, sloped backs, scruffy fur and clumsy gait, hyenas are not the most appealing creatures. They also have a dozen ways to make a horrible din and a miserable reputation as cowardly scavengers. But field studies have revealed hyenas to resort much more to hunting than scavenging for their food. They hunt with considerable intelligence and courage, even attacking rhinoceroses and young elephants. Lions are stronger than hyenas; they often steal the latter's kill and rely more on scavenging than the much-maligned hyena.

Grouped in tightly knit clans of up to 20 members, they live in a den with entrance holes connected by a network of tunnels. They mark out the clan territory with their dung and go on regular border patrols to keep out rival clans. Unusual among the mammals, the females are stronger and heavier than the males (70kg to the male's 58kg: 154 to 128lb). This evolution is thought to result from the mother's need to protect her young against the male's frequent cannibalistic tendencies.

Clan solidarity is constantly reinforced, particularly before a hunt, with some elaborate meeting ceremonies: they will sniff each other's mouths, necks and heads, raise a hind leg and lick each other before going off, reassured, on the group activity. Hunting is a carefully co-ordinated affair.

GRAZERS AND BROWSERS

The grasslands and bushlands of East Africa support the finest variety of herbivores in the world. In Kenya alone, there are more than 30 different species of antelope, ranging in size from the eland – the world's largest antelope – to the tiny Zanzibar duiker. Some of them graze (eat grass) indiscriminately; others graze selectively, choosing their habitat according to their diet; others graze and browse (eat the shoots and leaves of trees and shrubs); and a few are almost exclusively browsers.

Whatever they eat, all antelopes are ruminants – that is, they have several stomachs for fodder in varying stages of digestion and they reprocess already swallowed fodder by chewing the cud, like buffalos and domestic cattle.

All species are diurnal (active in the day), with a preference for mornings and evenings for feeding. Except for impala and some of the very small antelopes, most breed in a very narrow period, usually giving birth to their calves just before the rains. Antelopes rely on alertness and flight to escape their enemies – predators such as lions, leopards, cheetahs and hyenas.

Wildebeest

The ugly, ungainly-looking wildebeest has a dark brown/black body, an erect mane and a long whitish tail. Both sexes have horns, which are straight as calves, but forward-curving in the adult animal. Wildebeest are primarily grazers, found in herds. Their preferred habitat is open grassland, and they actively avoid areas with tall grass and dense vegetation, where they are very susceptible to being hunted. You are likely to see wildebeest in large numbers – possibly hundreds of thousands – if you visit the Maasai Mara when they are passing through on their annual migration between August and October. Watch out for them in single file as they make their dangerous path across the plains.

Giraffe

The giraffe has, it seems, achieved a state of grace, an ineffable dignity, just from being quite literally above it all – as much as 5m (16ft) for males. He relies on acute eyesight and his privileged vantage point to see potential dangers long before they arrive, fleeing instead of coping with them in a fight. The giraffe gets his liquid from juicy or dew-covered foliage, so as to avoid bending down to drink ground water in an ungainly split, vulnerable to attack from lions.

Females give birth standing up, and the calf, already almost 2m (6½ft) tall and weighing 65kg (143lb), is dropped, head first and with a thud, over a metre to the ground. The fall breaks the umbilical cord.

There are three main species: the reticulated giraffe, found only in northern Kenya, is bronze coloured with a distinct web-like pattern to its coat; the Maasai giraffe, which is smaller and darker with a ragged spot pattern; and the Rothschild giraffe, the tallest variety, whose coat pattern lies somewhere in between.

Reticulated giraffe

Zebra

The zebra herd consists of strong family units, in which a stallion stays together with up to six mares and their foals, and groups of male bachelors. The bachelor groups are quite frivolous,

Zebras crossing

spending most of their time racing, wrestling and generally fooling around. Relations between the stallion and his 'harem' are cordial, enhanced by mutual grooming. Unlike many animals, the zebra stallion is friendly and courteous to other stallions in the herd. When lions or hyenas threaten, the stallion just stands his ground, biting and kicking the aggressors to give his family plenty of time to escape. This ploy is quite often successful because lions prefer to rely on surprise attack, rather than a pitched battle, for making their kill.

Hippopotomus

Man is the hippo's only real threat, although a pride of lions will attack a solitary hippo on land, and crocodiles take the occasional baby hippo in the water. Females defend their young by making use of their long tusks (actually canine teeth). Despite their benign look, hippos probably account for more wildlife-induced human deaths than any other animal, including lions and snakes. They specialise in capsizing boats which get too near, either drowning or biting the people inside. Hippos are also dangerous on land at night, since they will run over anybody standing between them and the water.

Monkey

Though not strictly vegetarian, East Africa's monkeys should be mentioned here. Several species live in Kenya, but most of them are localised in their distribution – the blue monkey, for instance, in small pockets in the west of the country; the

De Brazza's monkey in forests on Mount Elgon and the Cherengani Range; the patas monkey in savannah country around Nanyuki, Rumuruti and Eldoret-Kitale; and the black-and-white colobus in highland forests.

One versatile monkey that is found throughout the country is the vervet (Cercopithecus aethiops), also known as green monkey, grivet, guenon and tantalus monkey. It is slight of build, agile and long-tailed, and always seen in noisy, bickering, family troops with lots of young animals. Both sexes are similar, although males are about 40 percent heavier, with conspicuous red, white and blue genital colouration.

Vervets generally inhabit well-wooded and well-watered grasslands but can also be found in semi-arid regions (usually near rivers or swamps) and evergreen forest edges at altitudes from sea-level to 4,000m (13,000ft). They are diurnal animals, although they may feed on moonlit nights. They

Hippos taking it easy in the Mara River

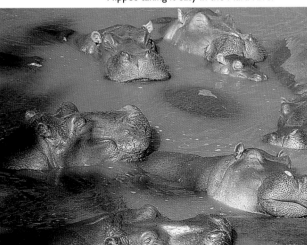

A baby baboon hitches a ride

have acute eyesight and excellent hearing, but a poor sense of smell. As well as vocal calls, they have a range of facial expressions, such as lowering their eyebrows, baring their teeth, raising or jerking their head.

Vervets are very gregarious and live in troops of six to 60 animals, sometimes reaching as many as 100. Troops comprise one or more adult males, adult females and young of all ages and sizes. Troops are territorial and defend their range against neighbouring troops with noisy group displays at the territory boundary.

Vervets are omnivorous with a predilection for vegetable matter. Their preferred tastes include fruits, flowers, grass seeds, shoots and bark, as well as insects, reptiles, small mammals, young birds and eggs.

Baboon

Behaviourists have used the baboon as an analogy for theorising about natural aggressiveness and male dominance among human beings. Quite apart from the dubious value of making such parallels, recent observations of baboons have shown them to be motivated not by fear and brutal tyranny, as had been claimed previously, rather by strong family relationships and social co-operation.

While the males play an important role in guaranteeing the safety of the baboon troop, it is the females who provide the group's stability. Females stay in the troop all their lives, while males are constantly on the move. Social cohesion is built around the family, with perhaps as many as 20 related units of mother and offspring. The males, for their part, form a separate band, moving on the outskirts of the group as it hunts for food.

You will often see male, female and baby baboons grooming each other. Their search for ticks, knots and dirt is an activity that reinforces group solidarity and what zoologists do not hesitate to call friendship. Male and female baboons form companionships independent of sexual mating. There is a definite hierarchy of prestige among female baboons, and the males seek some reflected glory by associating with the most prominent females – the troop's effective leaders who decide exactly when to move and which direction to take.

The baboons' diet consists of young shoots of savannah grass, shrubs and herbs, but their favourite food is fruit, especially figs. They occasionally turn carnivore and hunt down birds, hare and young gazelles. Indeed, nothing would be safe on an unguarded picnic.

Photography

Kenya's dramatic landscapes and awesome wildlife make it a photographer's heaven, and few people come without a camera. The safari vehicles and land cruisers have pop-up roofs to give you unimpeded standing shots while on game drives, although 'camera shake', from shooting from a moving vehicle, is common. A zoom of some kind is highly recommended for wildlife shots, otherwise, when you see your prints, you'll often find the animals have shrunk to the size of a pea. Most animals are shy and won't wait around to give you a perfect pose; the quickest photographer often gets the best shot.

People are another matter. Be sensitive to the various cultures you will come across; some tribes fear that a photo will capture their soul. Always ask permission before taking someone's photo, particularly Muslim women and tribes including the Maasai and Samburu. Some tribes will demand payment for posing.

BIRDS

The variety of birds is just as striking as the range of animals in Kenya. From the tiny sugarbird to the ostrich (at up to 2.75m/ 9ft the world's biggest bird, as well as one of the fastest – running at up to 70kph or 45mph), the range is so diverse that in many places it is possible to count over 400 species. In the savannah, as well as ostrich you'll see marabou storks, crested secretary birds and ground hornbill, plus various species of vulture, bustard, eagle, hawk, falcon, buzzard, vulturine guineafowl, black partridge, ox pecker, hoopoe and lapwing.

In addition to the birds of prey, brightly coloured touraco, toucan and owls can be seen in the forests, while storks, cranes, pelicans, flamingos, cormorants, ibis, hamerkops and fish eagles are usually plentiful on or by the lakes.

REPTILES

The richness of reptiles in East Africa compares favourably with any other part of the world. Reptiles have little commercial value in Kenya, so poaching is not a major problem. A few crocodiles are killed for their skins and smuggled out individually, but there is little trade in snakes and lizards. The Nile crocodile inhabits Kenya's rivers and lakes; it takes many human lives every year. Other reptiles to look out for include mamba snakes, puff adders, spitting cobras, tree snakes, rock pythons, vipers, geckos, and colourful agama lizards.

Colourful agama lizard

Cheetahs in Nairobi National Park, with the city behind

NAIROBI

Central Nairobi

In less than a century Kenya's capital, **Nairobi**, has grown from a remote railway outpost to become East Africa's largest city. Its modern skyline seems to announce its prominence as an international convention centre, a headquarters for multi-national businesses and United Nations bureaux and, not least, the safari capital of the world. Kenya's political, administrative, business and trade activities are all centred on this town.

Nairobi has the attendant problems of capital cities every-where: traffic, street crime and a rapidly growing population (estimated at around three million), many of whom are poor. But for thousands of visitors who pass through, preparing for the bush or resting up between safaris, the capital city is not an unpleasant place to be. At 1,660m (5,446ft) above sea level, Nairobi has an equatorial climate that is temperate all year round, with warm days and cool nights. There are plenty of restaurants, shops and service facilities and few mosquitoes.

In a country where hurry is not considered a virtue, the central streets of the city almost bustle. Most first-time visitors are unaware of the contrasts that lie between the shanty towns to the east and the landscaped homes of the northern and western suburbs. Instead, they notice the curious mixture of colonial legacy and African resurgence that makes up Nairobi.

In 1899, when builders of the Mombasa–Uganda railway line established a supply depot at Mile 327, the bleak, swampy riverside place that the Maasai called *enkare nyarobe* (sweet water) was nothing more than a campsite for hundreds of Indian labourers, and a few wooden shacks that housed the engineers who paused here to contemplate the difficulties of laying track across the Great Rift Valley. Soon, a frontier town emerged, with a central street (now Kenyatta Avenue) broad enough for a 12-span oxcart to wheel around.

Catching up on the news with *The Nation*

Three years later the place was nearly abandoned when plague swept the town, and a government decree had it burned to the ground. Despite another plague in 1904, Nairobi was rebuilt and by the time the Protectorate had officially moved its headquarters there from Mombasa in 1907, the white hunters were streaming in to embark on safaris from the newly opened Norfolk Hotel. The most prominent of them was Theodore Roosevelt, the US President, who headed a safari with 500 porters, all dressed in blue, and each carrying 25kg (55lb) of supplies. In ten months – while out of office – Roosevelt bagged no less than 296 animals.

Matatus on Nairobi's hectic highways

Meanwhile, the British government was strongly encouraging settlement of the Central Highlands, and Nairobi became the social and commercial centre for the growing white farming community. Indian traders developed the bazaar, while Africans came in from the villages to work as labourers. During World War II Nairobi served as a major garrison town, and much of the local game was killed to provide food for the troops. Thus, in 1947, the government formed the first of Kenya's many game sanctuaries, Nairobi National Park.

The building dominating the skyline, the **Kenyatta Conference Centre**, symbolises the interaction of the city's European origins and African destiny by combining a cylindrical skyscraper with a cone-shaped congress hall, reminiscent of tribal huts. A **statue of Jomo Kenyatta** sits alongside City Square, as do the old neoclassical Law Courts, the model of an English county court building.

White-columned arcades, the dominant architectural feature of the business district, are perfectly adapted to the climate, offering protection from the sudden rains or midday sun. They shelter the shops and restaurants along Mama

Ngina Street – formerly Queensway and named after Kenyatta's wife – and Kimathi Street, named after Dedan Kimathi, a Mau Mau leader executed by the British in 1957.

The long, broad **Kenyatta Avenue** runs west from the Stanley. A few blocks north along Muindi Mbingu Street, a rather more African hub of activity can be found around the City Market. You can browse through fragrant flower and produce stalls in the main hall, but keep a tight hold on your valuables. The curio stands offer good bargains on soapstone, wood carvings and other handicrafts – if you can endure the overbearing stallholders. Across from the market is the Arabian-style Jamia Mosque, built in 1933 by the Sunni sect.

Skull of Homo erectus,
Nairobi's National Museum

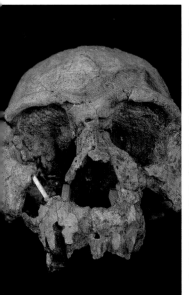

The **National Museum**, on Museum Hill at the northern end Uhuru Highway, has recently undergone a major transformation and deserves a visit above all for its great prehistoric collection depicting the origins of man and various animals. On exhibition here is a replica of No. 1470, the skull belonging to our 2.5 million-year-old ancestor discovered at Lake Turkana. You can also view the findings from Olduvai Gorge in Tanzania: fossilised remains, 1.65 million years old, of Homo habilis, the first tool-making man, with his stone hand-axes and cleavers; as well as Homo erectus, a 1.15-million-year-old man coming closer to the brain capacity of Homo sapiens.

The remains of prehistoric animals include a giant ostrich, rhinoceros and elephant; on a smaller scale are bird, insect and butterfly collections. In the courtyard is a stuffed model of Ahmed, the legendary elephant from Marsabit, who was declared a national monument by Kenyatta in 1970 and placed under 24-hour guard to protect him from poachers. He died of natural causes four years later, aged around 60, with each tusk weighing a mighty 67kg (148lb).

Across from the museum is the Snake House and aquariums, where you can safely view those creatures you hope never to see in the wild: the deadly green mamba, black mamba, puff adder and red spitting cobra.

City Outskirts

If you are visiting Nairobi before you set off for the national parks and game reserves, a tour of the **Nairobi National Park** makes a good introduction. It has a beautifully varied landscape of forest, hills and savannah. Although Nairobi's well-marked, smooth-surfaced roads may seem a little tame if you've already visited other parks, the sight of wildlife grazing against the backdrop of the city skyline is still impressive.

There are lots of lions, and the gate keepers at the park entrance may tell you where they are to be found. While the park has no elephants, it does offer one of the best chances to see rhino, due to the black rhino sanctuary located here. Also look out for the ostriches, warthogs, baboons, zebras, giraffes and impalas. Although the animals are fenced off on one side of the park from the Nairobi–Mombasa highway, they have free access for migration to and from Amboseli and Tsavo across the Athi and Kaputei Plains. If you have missed some of the animals at the other parks and reserves because they were too shy, you will find them blasé about vehicles here.

At the western end of the park is the **Safari Walk and Animal Orphanage**, founded in 1963 to provide a home for young animals injured or deserted in the wild. Zoologists who care for them until they can be returned to the reserves have a chance to study these animals up close. It's a good place for children to have their first easy look at Kenya's wildlife, but for adults it may seem little more than a glorified zoo and has a fairly limited appeal.

National Independence Monument

En route to the park you will probably pass Kenya's majestic **National Independence Monument** in the Uhuru Gardens. It was erected on the site where the British government passed the papers of independence to the Kenyan people on 12 December 1963. A second monument marks the 25th anniversary of that day. And just off the Langata Road is another Nairobi institution, the **Carnivore Restaurant** (see page 139).

The Bomas of Kenya, a few kilometres away, offers a chance to see traditional tribal dances performed by the Harambee Dancers, a professional dance group. Many find the two-hour show – performed in a circular arena with an inferior sound system – too long, but it does feature a variety of Kenyan dance styles and traditional instruments you'll be unlikely to see elsewhere. Still, if it proves too much, you can always go and explore the grounds, which are laid out with the traditional homesteads (bomas) of various tribes, and peruse the crafts for sale.

To meet orphaned elephants and rhinos up close, visit the **David Sheldrick Wildlife Trust** situated just inside the Nairobi National Park through the Mbagathi Gate off the Magadi Road. Feeding time is at 11am sharp.

The nearby **Giraffe Centre**, on Koitobos Road off Langata South Road, was founded in 1978 to save the Rothschild's giraffe from extinction. Though the aim of the centre is to teach children about wildlife conservation, most adults enjoy the chance to hand-feed the giraffes as much as the kids do.

Another popular excursion is to the **Karen Blixen Museum**, the homestead where the author (pen name Isak Dinesan) lived and ran her coffee farm from 1917 to 1931. After the grandeur of the Hollywood film *Out of Africa (see page 18),* which was shot here, the first thing that strikes you about the house is how small it is. The beautiful wood-panelled rooms have been restored and filled with original artefacts and reproductions. From the pretty gardens you can gaze over the Ngong Hills, where Karen Blixen's lover, Denys Finch Hatton, is buried.

Just west of the city centre is the suburb of Westlands with three shopping centres, assorted shops and a variety of restaurants offering international cuisine. Heading north of the city on Forest Road is Africa's first traditional Hindu Temple, **Shree Swaminarayan Mandir**, with intricate wooden and stone ceilings, pillars, walls and windows. On Limuru Road at Gigiri are the headquarters of the **United Nations**. A few minutes' drive from here is the **Village Market**, a shopping centre and leisure complex that is home to a popular Friday 'Maasai Market'.

THE CENTRAL HIGHLANDS

The Central Highlands lie north of Nairobi, a fertile agricultural region whose highlights are the Aberdare National Park and Mount Kenya. In colonial days European settlers took much of the best land here for themselves, and the area became known as the 'White Highlands'. Today, however, the land is farmed by the native Kikuyu. The drive north from Nairobi is a pretty one past thatched huts, lush slopes of coffee trees and assorted horticultural produce. If you travel on a Tuesday or Saturday, stop by the open-air market at Karatina, about 20km (12 miles) before Nyeri, the centre of the region.

Giant groundsel on Mount Kenya

Aberdare National Park

The Aberdare Mountains, which form the steep eastern edge of the Rift Valley, were named after the Victorian president of the Royal Geographical Society, Lord Aberdare. Although the Kikuyu name, 'Nyandarua', has been officially restored, it has been slow to catch on. This impressive range is rich in wildlife and contains one of the country's largest protected forest areas and water catchment for Nairobi.

Due to the dense vegetation, it is not always easy to catch sight of the animals while driving through the park. The best way to see them is to visit one of the purpose-built game-viewing lodges. Guests are driven from a base hotel in Nyeri or Mweiga (The Outspan for Treetops or Aberdare Country Club for the Ark) to the forest lodges, where they can watch the parade of wildlife around a watering hole.

Karatina market

Treetops, on the eastern edge of the park, is the original 'tree hotel', literally built on stilts in a forest clearing. It started as a single cabin in 1932 for a few guests who would go there on moonlit nights to see the wild animals wander over to the waterhole and natural salt lick. Twenty years later, the hotel welcomed Princess Elizabeth and the Duke of Edinburgh as guests on their honeymoon. During their stay, news came of the death of King George VI and Elizabeth's ascension to the English throne. In 1954 Mau Mau rebels burned Treetops to the ground, but it was rebuilt three years later.

The Ark, built to look like Noah's vessel, lies at a higher altitude in the middle of the forest. It is considered by many to be the better of the two lodges for game viewing; lions frequent the waterhole and the elusive leopard and rare bongo are occasionally sighted here.

Some 40km (25 miles) north of Nyeri, on the Laikipia plains, a different game-viewing experience awaits at **Sweetwaters Tented Camp**. The camp is situated in the Ol Pejeta Conservancy, part of a 18,015ha (110,000-acre) ranch that once belonged to the arms billionaire Adnan Kashoggi. Ol Pejeta is a peaceful retreat on flat, open savannah land that is good for game spotting. The camp specialises in night game

Luxury tented accommodation at Sweetwaters

drives, which are not allowed in Kenya's national parks, and there is also a rhino and chimp sanctuary on the conservancy.

Nyahururu

At 2,360m (7,742ft) **Nyahururu** (Thompson's Falls) is Kenya's highest town, set almost on the equator. Its waterfall is named after the explorer Joseph Thompson, who discovered it in 1883. The falls are a popular stop-off point for tourists, though the 70m (230ft) cascade is pretty rather than dramatic, and the serenity of the surrounding forest is somewhat marred by the pestering of the curio sellers here. You can climb to the foot of the falls, but there is only one safe way down, and occasional muggings have occurred on the path. The best plan is to enquire at Thompson's Falls Lodge for a guide.

The **equator** is proclaimed by a yellow marker that states 'This Sign is on the Equator'. You'll no doubt be hassled by a 'guide' with a funnel and a bucket of water, who will demonstrate how water swirls clockwise down a drain north of the equator and anti-clockwise south of it.

Mount Kenya National Park

Africa's second highest mountain, **Mount Kenya**, is an extinct volcano lying on the equator. The snow-capped twin peaks – Batian at 5,199m (17,058ft) and Nelion at 5,188m (17,022ft) – were named after two 19th-century Maasai ritual chiefs. Mount Kenya is the exponent of a remarkable natural phenomenon; the German missionary-explorer Johann Ludwig Krapf was mocked when he reported snowfields on the equator in 1849, but Joseph Thompson confirmed the phenomenon some 34 years later. In fact, Mount Kenya is the only point around the globe to have continuous equatorial snow.

The two highest peaks are regularly scaled by experienced climbers, though few make it to the top. A third peak, Lenana, at 4,985m (16,354ft) is known as 'Tourist Peak' because it is a relatively easy climb. The preferred entry point for a climb is Naro Moru, on the western side. The walk is a botanist's delight. The dense forest changes to bamboo jungle at 2,500m (8,200ft) and then, at 3,000m (9,840ft) to clearings surrounded by charming Abyssinian Hagenia trees hung with orchids, old-man's beard and several other creepers.

Mountain Sickness

More people die of pulmonary oedema on Mount Kenya each year than on any other mountain. It is caused by an accumulation of water on the lungs. The symptoms are headaches, nausea, sleeplessness, loss of appetite, swelling and fluid retention, breathing difficulties, slurred speech and abnormal behaviour. The only cure is to get to a lower altitude – as quickly as possible. To avoid pulmonary oedema, allow time to get accustomed to the altitude before going higher up.

But there are much easier ways to enjoy Mount Kenya, with the **Serena Mountain Lodge** *(see page 131)* lying at the southwestern edge of the massif inside Mount Kenya National Park and offering the best spot for game viewing.

The **Mount Kenya Safari Club** *(see page 130)* is a luxurious landmark on the mountain's northwestern side. If you can't splurge on a night here, treat youself to the buffet lunch and marvel at this equatorial oasis set against the mountain backdrop. You can also visit the adjacent **Mount Kenya Game Ranch and Animal Orphanage**, which has successfully bred the rare African bongo, a forest antelope with brown and white stripes, seldom seen in the wild.

Samburu, Buffalo Springs and Shaba Reserves

The Samburu and Buffalo Springs National Reserves are the northernmost of the popular game parks. At 300 sq km (116 sq miles), the area is small by Kenyan standards. Its attraction lies in the beauty of the landscape and the concentration of wildlife, including several species not found outside this region. Shaba National Reserve is 9km (5.5 miles) to the east of Buffalo Springs on the other side of the road.

The reserves are roughly a two-hour drive north of Nanyuki. The tarmac ends at Isiolo, a service town with a mixed community of native Borans and Somali Muslims. There is a police checkpoint at the end of town, where you must register your destination and fend off the harmless but assertive jewellery sellers who besiege the tourist vans. The checkpoint is there to act as a safeguard against Somali bandits, called *shiftas*, who once waged a border dispute over Kenya's northern territory.

Once past the checkpoint, the bumpy dirt road enters the land of the Samburu, a pastoral tribe related to the Maasai. Tall and slender, they resemble the Maasai in native dress and decorative jewellery, and the hair of the warriors is styled with ochre-coloured clay. Several villages consisting of low huts made of woven branches coated with mud and sisal mats lie on the outskirts of the reserves, and you will see many Samburu tending their herds of goats and cattle.

The Ewaso Nyiro River divides the two reserves, with Samburu on the north bank and Buffalo Springs on the south. No river in Kenya is free from crocodiles, and this one has its fair share of particularly large, impressive ones.

Samburu National Reserve receives a steady stream of  visitors, and there are several upmarket lodges and luxury tented camps for accommodation. The wild, acacia-dotted landscape surrounds Koitogor Mountain in the middle of the reserve, while the red granite outcrop of Ololokwe rises outside the northern boundary.

Buffalo Springs is named after the underground springs here, which were uncovered by the British army in the 1960s, when they blew out a 12-m- (40-ft-) wide hole. The natural

Samburu mother and child at Buffalo Springs

pool created by this event is one of the few places in the reserve where you can get out of your vehicle and swim safely, making it a popular picnic spot, with superb views across the marsh to the Wamba Mountains.

Shaba National Reserve was established at the same time as Samburu and Buffalo Springs. The northern area stretches 34km (21 miles) along the Ewaso Ngiro River with a number of springs and swampy areas. The rugged Shaba Hill dominates the southern part of the reserve. The well-appointed Sarova Shaba Lodge is an oasis in the bush with a natural spring cascading through the main buildings, and Joy's Camp, situated at Joy Adamson's original campsite, also overlooks a spring.

Grevy's zebra, seen only in the north

Animals migrate freely between the three reserves, as do the guests on their daily game drives. Of special interest is the Grevy's zebra, which is larger than the common zebra, with thin stripes, trumpet-shaped ears and a white belly. It is not found outside northern Kenya, nor is the reticulated giraffe, which roams the area in large numbers. The highly distinctive bronze, web-patterned coat and white markings of the reticulated giraffe make it the most handsome of the three varieties *(see page 37)*. Other rare species endemic to this area include the Beisa oryx, the blue-legged (male) Somali ostrich and the gerenuk, also know as the giraffe gazelle because of its long neck, slender frame and its habit of standing on its hind legs to nibble at tree branches.

THE GREAT RIFT VALLEY

The **Great Rift Valley** is part of a geological fault that runs across Africa from the Zambezi Delta in Mozambique to the Jordan Valley. It was formed in the Pleistocene era, when the collision of two parallel plates thrust the harder rock upwards, while the softer rock dropped nearly 1,000m (around 3,280ft) to form a wide trench bottom. The resulting chain of lakes and extinct volcanic cones that run along the Rift

The broad Rift Valley, with Mount Longonot in the distance

Valley, as it cuts through the highlands and descends into the Maasai Plains, makes it Kenya's most distinguishing topographical feature.

Many safari holidays feature a visit to one or two of the Rift Valley lakes, which stretch out along a north–south axis from Lake Turkana in the far north to Lake Magadi, which is completely dry and the source of the world's largest soda deposits. Those with a special interest in bird-watching should plan to spend a little more time in this area, as over 450 resident and migratory species have been recorded around the central lakes.

The lakes lie in the valley floor, surrounded by a fairly tame landscape of farmland in the south and overgrazed scrubland further north. There are several good viewpoints overlooking the Rift Valley – particularly the one facing the dormant volcano, Mount Longonot – along the eastern escarpment on the main road north from Nairobi. The most dramatic landscape, seemingly more characteristic of the Rift

Valley's turbulent past, is along the C51 highway between Marigat and Eldoret. It climbs through the pretty sculpted shapes of the Tugen Hills to Kabarnet before dropping down sharply through the Kerio Valley and back up again along the high, twisted roads and spectacular vistas of the Elgeyo Escarpment. At Iten the scenery and road conditions change abruptly as you cross a high plateau to Eldoret.

Lake Naivasha

The closest lake to Nairobi, **Lake Naivasha** is as much a weekend retreat for city residents as a stop-over for tourists. At 1,890m (6,201ft) it is the highest of the Rift Valley lakes. The reed-rimmed shoreline, with its floating clumps of papyrus, changes constantly with the fluctuating water level. You can fish for black bass and tilapia, but the main attraction of this freshwater lake is its birdlife, which is best observed on a boat trip to the wildlife sanctuary on Crescent Island. The island is actually the outer rim of a volcanic crater that forms the deepest part of the lake. Here, as at all of Kenya's lakes, take extra precautions against mosquitoes from dusk to dawn. The mighty, yellow-barked acacias around the lake were called 'fever trees' by the early settlers who thought they were somehow responsible for malaria. In fact, both the trees and mosquito larvae thrive near large bodies of water.

Formerly Maasai country, the irrigated, agricultural land around the lake is still largely owned by Europeans. It is used to grow vegetables and flowers, mainly for export.

Hell's Gate National Park

A few kilometres down South Lake Road is **Hell's Gate National Park**. Though small in area – 68 sq km (26 sq miles) – the landscape is impressive, with some spectacular rock formations and steep, fiery basalt cliffs enclosing vast stretches of open grassland. This is one of the few parks where you can leave your vehicle and explore the area on foot. The volcanic pinnacle called Fischer's Tower, named after an early German explorer, marks the entrance to the gorge. There is a warden's post and information centre about 11km (7 miles) in from the Elsa Gate, where a nature trail leads to Ol Basta, a second volcanic plug. The clouds of steam emitted from the adjacent ridgetop mark the Olkaria Geothermal Station.

Although they had not been spotted for several years, a pair of rare lammergeier vultures has now bred and is numbered among the many raptors nesting in the cliffs. Giraffe, impala, hartebeest, zebra and Grant's and Thomson's gazelle all graze in the grasslands among the whistling acacia thorn bushes, along with buffalo and the majestic eland.

Lake Nakuru

Lake Nakuru is famous for the multitude of flamingos that flock here to feed on the algae. The lake has no outlet and so minerals build up, giving the water a high alkaline content. Algae thrive on it, and so in turn do the flamingos.

In earlier years up to two million birds would mass here at one time, covering the entire surface of the lake. In the late 1970s, and again in the mid-1990s, however, a period of exceptionally heavy rainfall raised the water level, causing a corresponding decrease in the water's alkalinity. The flamingos dispersed to other lakes in the Rift Valley, primarily Lake Bogaria. When the lake receded to its original size, the birds failed to return in their earlier numbers. Nevertheless,

Flamingo facts

There are two main species of flamingo: the Greater Flamingo – taller and white – and the Lesser Flamingo, which is unique to the Rift Valley and greatly outnumbers its larger cousin. The pink hue of the flamingo's white features is caused by a carotene pigment in the algae.

many thousands of them can usually be seen spreading out in a dainty pink ribbon along the shoreline. A large number of pelicans also fish for tilapia in the lake.

Lake Nakuru National Park surrounds the lake, a mixed landscape of acacia woodland and rocky cliffs. It provides a habitat for over 450 species of bird, lion, leopard, jackal and Rothschild's giraffe, among many others. Black and white rhino have been translocated from other parts of the country in the hope that they will breed successfully to restock other national parks. To protect them from poachers, an electric fence has been erected around the park's entire perimeter, and wardens patrol the park.

Watch out for the huge pythons that inhabit the dense woodland areas between the lakeshore and the cliffs. Hippo Point has a far less threatening group of hippos, although it is extremely difficult to drive near to, as the land around

Lake Nakuru flamingos

it is muddy and unstable. In addition, the picnic site at the top of the Baboon Cliffs offers a panoramic view looking out across the lake.

Lake Bogoria

After the drive through the sun-baked landscape broken only by goats scavenging along the roadside and termite mounds rising like sandcastles between the bushes, the waters of **Lake Bogoria**, lying to the south of Lake Baringo, may seem like a mirage. Early explorers who discovered it on their expeditions to Uganda described it as the most beautiful view in Africa, and, indeed, the sight of Bogoria's steaming geysers set against the backdrop of the lake's rocky precipices is quite magnificent.

A local legend claims that the lake was formed when the god Chebet, angered by the meanness of the Kamale tribe towards passing travellers, invoked a deluge that lasted for days and wiped out their village. Lake Bogoria is still called 'the place of the lost tribe'.

Although the steaming springs may well look like the fury of the gods, they are actually the remnants of past volcanic activity. You can get out of your car for a closer look at the sulphurous pools, which bubble like a cauldron.

Termite mound, Lake Bogoria

Brave picnickers have been known to boil their eggs in the water. However, great care should be taken when walking near the springs, as the earth's crust is very thin, with scalding water simmering just below the surface. This area is very remote, and it's a long way to the nearest burns unit.

Like Lake Nakuru, Bogoria's waters are alkaline, and if you haven't seen many flamingos at Nakuru, you'll

probably find them here. Bogoria has outdistanced Nakuru in the flamingo count in recent years, with up to half a million gathering at a time. Over 350 other bird species have also been recorded here.

Special kudu game drives and bird-watching tours can be arranged at the Lake Bogoria Hotel, which you will find just outside the Loboi Gate. In addition, there are three campsites on the southern side of the lake.

Lake Baringo

The northernmost of the central Rift Valley lakes, **Baringo** is a freshwater lake with abundant stocks of tilapia, catfish and other colourful vertebrates. The cloudy, brown colour of the water comes from the deposits of topsoil washed down the river during the rains; this erosion also accounts for its shallowness – over its entire 168 sq km (65 sq miles) it is no deeper than 12m (39ft).

Hippos wallow throughout the lake and graze on its shore at night, often wandering fearlessly on to the lawns of the

Njemps tribeswoman with colourful beaded jewellery

Lake Baringo Club, the only lodge on the lakeshore. Crocodiles are also numerous, but do not reach any great size here.

With some 470 species recorded around the lake, the area is a bird-lover's paradise. **Gibraltar (Lesukut) Island** has the largest nesting colony of goliath herons, the tallest of the species at 1.5m (5ft). Herons, Verreaux's eagle, great white egrets, and a wide variety of hornbills are other star attractions. A resident ornithologist at the lodge leads morning bird-walks along the nearby escarpment and evening walks along the lakeshore. You may ask him all about the local winged residents. A stay at Baringo Island Camp on Ol Kokwa Island includes a number of watersport activities, hiking, birdwatching and fabulous views over the lake to the edges of the Rift Valley.

Hour-long boat trips out on the lake are available at the lodge, but they're expensive. You'll see the magnificent fish eagles that swoop down over the water and snatch up a fish, plus hippos, herons, monitor lizards and other wildlife on the shores of the islands.

You can make another excursion to a Njemps village, a small tribe related to the Maasai, where you'll see the lifestyle of a man, his three wives and 18 children.

WESTERN KENYA

Western Kenya is not a common destination on the tourist trail. But for the return visitor to Kenya, or maybe for those who have the time and the interest to look beyond the game parks and beach resorts, it offers an amazing diversity of environments, from swamp land to mountain wilderness, equatorial rainforest and the sultry shores of Lake Victoria.

Much of western Kenya is heavily populated, with fertile farmland and several small, busy market towns. The bulk of Kenya's tea plantations and sugar cane fields are found in this region. The Luo are the largest ethnic group, occupying the lowlands along the lakeshore, followed by the Luyha in the area north of Kisumu, the Nandi around Eldoret, the Kipsigis in the Kericho district and the Gush in the Kisii hills.

Dusty, noisy **Eldoret** is one of the fastest growing towns in Kenya. There is little to do or see here, but the tourist class hotels, banks and post office make it an adequate stop-over en route to more interesting places in the area.

Saiwa Swamp National Park

Kenya's smallest national park, **Saiwa Swamp**, is worth a visit to admire the unique ecological habitat confined with in its 200ha (500 acres). The park was created in 1984 to protect the sitatunga (pronounced 'statunga'), a semi-aquatic antelope that is only found in this area. This small, reddish-brown creature spends most of the day submerged in the water with only the tip of its nose sticking out. It emerges to feed in the early morning and late afternoon, dipping down again at the slightest inkling of danger. You can spy on it from the cover of a tree-hide overlooking the swamp .

The boggy terrain is caused by the run-off from Mount Elgon. You can easily explore the trails in two to three hours and in normal footwear, as walkways and bridges have been built over the swamp. It is a delightful walk through indige-nous rainforest. Vervet, colobus and the white-bearded Brazza monkeys crash through the high branches overhead. From the five observation towers, you can look out over the swamp and catch sight of the many bird species, which number over 300.

Mount Elgon National Park

Mount Elgon has been called 'Kenya's loneliest park', and this extinct volcano straddling the Ugandan border is indeed remote. Lower than Mount Kenya, but with greater bulk, it has similar vegetation and wildlife. The southeastern slopes of the mountain actually fall within the boundaries of Mount Elgon National Park. During the rainy months, the roads are impassable and the upper slopes are hidden in the clouds, making December to March the best time to visit. For those prepared to make the journey, the rewards are great: im-pressive cliffs, hot springs, mountain streams, massive trees and dense forest provide some of the best hiking in the whole of Kenya. A climb to Koitoboss Peak and the hot springs at Suam Gorge (which lie in Uganda) is also possible.

Of greatest interest to most visitors are the elephant caves – the most famous of which is Kitum – on the lower slopes in-side the park. These huge caves extend horizontally into the mountain and are thought to have been carved out by elephant tusks. Amazingly, the giant pachyderms make their way up the rocky forest slopes to gouge lumps of sodium from this mas-sive, natural salt lick. You can see the tusk marks on the cave walls. If you arrive early in the morning, you may still be able to catch some animals at the salt licks before they retreat into the forest. When walking up to the caves, keep an eye out for buffalo or giant forest hogs; take care also when entering the caves themselves. Should you wish to explore the depths of the caves, you will need a strong torch. Note, too, that there are scores of (harmless) fruit bats hanging from the roof.

Because of Mount Elgon's remote position on the Ugandan border, there have been security problems in the past with armed rebels and elephant poachers. Although things have calmed down in recent years, it is a good idea to assess the situation locally before setting off up the mountain. You should be safe enough in the park itself, as rangers at the gate will be able to offer advice and an escort if necessary.

Kakamega Forest National Reserve

Situated to the north of Kisumu, **Kakamega Forest National Reserve** is Kenya's only remaining equatorial rainforest.

Once part of a vast, continental tract that stretched to the Atlantic Ocean, the 238 sq-km (92 sq-mile) reserve now attracts both nature experts and scientists as well as tourists to explore this isolated environment, one which no longer exists elsewhere in East Africa. A local guide can help you make the most of your visit by explaining the forest ecosystem and identifying some of the unique trees and plants found here, as well as the resident wildlife. Colourful butterflies and around 330 different bird species have established themselves in the forest, including the great blue turaco and crowned eagle.

The lush Kakamega Forest National Reserve

Kisumu and Lake Victoria

The broad, clean streets and white buildings of **Kisumu** are a pleasant surprise for the travel-weary. In this languid, lake-side town you can go about your business without too many hassles from the beggars and souvenir sellers you encounter elsewhere. Either it's just too hot to bother, or this inland port, which has long served as a crossroads for African, Asian and European traders, takes foreigners for granted.

In 1901 the railway line finally reached Port Florence, as the town was then called, completing a trade link with Uganda across the lake. Considerable heat, high levels of humidity, as well as outbreaks of sleeping sickness, malaria and blackwater fever made it the least desirable posting in the British Empire. However, by the start of World War II it had become a major East African transportation hub and administrative centre. Kenya's third-largest city fell into decline with the disbanding of the East African Community in 1977 and the drop in lake traffic. Today it has a mixed aura of charm

Rusinga Island

Rusinga is the best known of Lake Victoria's small islands. A wealth of prehistoric fossils have been found here, including Mary Leakey's discovery of the skull Proconsul africonus, an early man-like ape. Rusinga was also the birthplace of one of Kenya's greatest statesmen, Tom Mboya. A Luo politician beloved by many Kenyans, he was assassinated by Kikuyu gunmen in 1969 to the detriment of the whole country.

You can reach the island by ferry or overland via a new causeway. Alternatively, take a flying safari, operated by Private Wilderness or Governor's Camp in the Maasai Mara. You'll be flown from your nearest airstrip for a half-day fishing trip or overnight excursion at the Rusinga Island Lodge or Mfangano Island Camp. The boat trip across the lake is great fun, even if you don't want to fish.

Dhow near Rusinga Island

and decay, and even an air of optimism as light industry replaces the rusting ships and empty warehouses along the shore.

Highly recommended is a visit to the **Kisumu Museum**, a short walk or ride east of town. An incredible specimen of taxidermy stands, on its forelegs, in the main exhibition hall: a frantic wildebeest with an attacking lioness clinging to its back. Less dramatic, but equally interesting are the collections of musical instruments displayed here. (You will also see toys and other traditional artefacts of West Kenyan ethnic groups.) The museum grounds contain a Luo homestead, a rather uninspiring aquarium, a turtle pond, crocodile pit and a snake house that is brighter than the one in Nairobi.

In the town itself, Kisumu's market is delightful, the largest in western Kenya and a good place to find a bargain. But the real attraction is **Lake Victoria**, the second-largest freshwater lake in the world. The main roads are set inland from the water's edge, so you can't really stroll along the shore. Swim-

Tea-picker near Kericho

ming is absolutely out of the question, as bilharzia, a nasty parasite, is present in the water. The best way to enjoy the lake is to take a boat trip or ferry from the dock to one of the small islands.

Kericho

Before or after your trip to Maasai Mara *(see page 71)*, particularly if you've spent a long time on the hot, dry and dusty road, you may find yourself, for the first time in your life, crying out for rain. There's one place that guarantees satisfaction – **Kericho** with its famous tea plantations about 250km (155 miles) northwest of Nairobi. Almost every day, at 3pm, dark clouds gather and burst into refreshing showers.

You can enjoy this spectacle from the comfort of your armchair at the **Tea Hotel**, where the unmistakable Englishness of the immaculate green lawns and flower gardens is a welcome change from the arid, red savannah. Built in 1952 as a clubhouse for the Brooke Bond tea company, to stay at the hotel is to take a delightful step back in time. The place is a swansong of the colonial era, and the rooms have their original 1950s-style furnishings. Afternoon tea is served on the patio or in the sitting room with its chintz curtains and kitschy furniture.

The **tea plantations** are well worth a visit. There are kilometres of lush green bushes packed in a shoulder-high carpet dotted with the heads of tea-pickers plucking the buds and topmost young leaves and tossing them into wicker baskets on their backs. With advance arrangements, you can also visit the tea factories on estates near the town for an explanation of the cutting, fermenting and drying stages in tea processing.

Kenya's tea industry prospered in the 1920s when experts decided that the soil here was perfect for producing the best-quality tea from Ceylonese and Indian plants. It is an example of how the British Empire functioned as a gigantic holding company, enabling the transfer of whole industries from one continent to another. Today, the Kericho plantations cover 15,000ha (37,000 acres), and the tea industry as a whole lies just behind tourism as Kenya's main foreign income earner.

Maasai Mara

If your trip to Kenya allows you time to visit only one game park, make it this one. The **Maasai Mara**, an extension of Tanzania's Serengeti National Park, gives you the best chance of seeing all the major wild animals in a superb rolling land-

The Maasai

The Maasai is Kenya's most famous tribe. This proud, nomadic people once ruled, through sheer ferocity, the fertile grasslands of the Rift Valley and the plains from Lake Turkana to Kilimanjaro. For centuries, they have herded cattle in search of water and fresh pasture, clinging to ancient traditions and resisting the encroachment of modern life.

Several related families live together in low, circular huts (manyattas) constructed by the women out of mud mixed with cow dung. Their diet consists of milk, maize and blood extracted from their cattle, which they rarely use for meat. The size of a Maasai's herd is a symbol of his wealth. The Maasai believe that God gave them all the cows in the world; the other animals belong to God and must not be harmed; only eland and buffalo, the 'wild cattle', can occasionally be hunted for food.

The Maasai are polygamous and practise the circumcision and initiation rites that take a male from boyhood to warrior status. Despite conflict with the authorities, the proud, young morani, who carry clubs, swords and spears, still see the killing of a lion as a test of manhood.

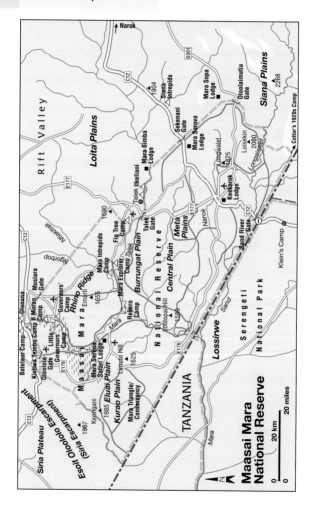

Maasai Mara National Reserve

scape of gentle hills and majestic acacia woodland.

This is one of the few places left in Africa where you can see animal herds roaming the plains in the vast numbers that early explorers once witnessed. Between the end of July and November, over one and a half million wildebeest, accompanied by half again as many zebras and gazelles, migrate from the Serengeti Plains to fresh pasture in the grasslands of the Mara, creating one of nature's grandest spectacles. Moving in groups of up to 20,000 at a time, they thunder across the plateau, hesitating one second at the

Ballooning over the Maasai Mara

Mara River until the pressure of their numbers forces the leaders to plunge into the swirling waters. Many perish before reaching the opposite bank, drowning in the rushing river or victims of the waiting crocodiles.

The Mara has the largest population of lions in Kenya, and you'll have the best chance of spotting a leopard in the wild here. The waters of the Talek and Mara rivers are abundant with hippo and there are large herds of elephant and buffalo.

The Mara is Maasai country; Mara, in fact, is a Maasai word meaning 'spotted' or 'mottled', a reference to the acacia trees dotting the plains. The 1,670- sq-km (645-sq-mile) area is a national game reserve, and Maasai herdsmen are permitted to reside with their cattle on parts of the land.

Mara zebra

While you do have the opportunity here to seek out the more elusive game, you must be careful not to drive too close or disturb the animals and their prey. It is advisable to have a four-wheel-drive vehicle and to enrol the help of a guide who knows the area.

The recently established **Mara Conservancy** manages the western part of the reserve, the Mara Triangle. This has brought together conservation professionals and the local Maasai communities, clamped down on poaching and restored roads and buildings. There are separate fees and guidelines for the Conservancy.

The remoteness of Maasai Mara adds to its adventure. Flying is the most convenient way to get there, and there are several small airstrips serving the lodges with daily flights from Nairobi. Though the 260-km (160-mile) drive across the Rift Valley from Nairobi is scenic in parts, the roads into the park from Narok or Kericho are atrocious after heavy rain, so be prepared to push. The main tarmac road to Narok and beyond is also in bad condition. Accommodation is plentiful, with lodges, permanent tented camps and a number of campsites.

THE SOUTHEAST

Two of the country's best-known parks are located in this area: Amboseli, famed for its elephant herds, which can be seen against a photographic backdrop of a snow-capped Kilimanjaro; and the vast Tsavo, the country's largest national park, split into East and West.

Amboseli National Park

Amboseli National Park is relatively small and can easily be covered in a day – hence it receives heavy tourist traffic: short-term visitors dashing down from Nairobi and safari vehicles trekking through to nearby Tsavo. On the positive side, hordes of roving tourists make a poacher's job difficult, and, as a result, Amboseli is Kenya's foremost elephant park, with some of the country's finest mature specimens. The sight of a herd of 40 or more or these creatures with the mellow evening sun setting over **Mount Kilimanjaro** *(see page 10)*  is truly impressive.

Amboseli's environment is a precarious one. Its swamps provided the Maasai with a natural watering hole until the land was declared a national park in 1973. By then the combination of overgrazing and increased tourism had turned vast areas into near desert, and a sudden rise in the water

Cooking on Kilimanjaro

table brought toxic salts to the surface, killing many trees. Extensive damage has also been caused by too much off-road driving. Lake Amboseli dried up to little more than a puddle for many years. Then, unseasonal torrents of rain in January 1993 flooded the park. It's unlikely that this popular park will ever get the breathing space it needs to fully recover. Amboseli serves as a reminder of the fragility of a seemingly rugged landscape.

Tsavo National Park

Tsavo is the largest national park in Kenya. Its territory of 20,800 sq km (8,030 sq miles) has been split into two separately controlled parks, divided by the Nairobi–Mombasa highway. Vast elephant herds once roamed the plains of Tsavo, along with the largest population of black rhino in Africa, numbering in the high thousands. However, in the

Acacia trees in the Tsavo East

past three decades or so, over three-quarters of the elephants and nearly all of the rhino have been wiped out by successive droughts and ruthless poaching.

The Kenyan government's anti-poaching forces, strongly focused on Tsavo, have been largely successful in stopping the slaughter. However, the whole northern sector of Tsavo East has been closed to the public as park rangers wage their war against the armed poachers.

Marabou stork in the Tsavo

The surviving elephant families, now tragically devoid of elders, tend to congregate near the park lodges and roads for safety, making them easy to see and photograph. The rhino sanctuary in Tsavo West shelters most of the remaining rhino, though you may still spot one in the wild in the Rhino Valley between the park's two lodges. The rest of the Big Five are well represented, and these, along with the wealth of other wildlife from the ubiquitous Marabou stork to the rare lesser kudu, account for Tsavo's popularity as a game-viewing mecca.

Tsavo West

Tsavo West has the most spectacular landscape, an undulating plain peppered with green hills and rounded buttes which are a legacy from the area's recent geological past. The nearby Chyulu Hills were created by volcanic action less than 500 years ago, and the Shetani Lava Flow on their southern edge is only 200 to 300 years old. There are trails leading across the lava rock to the top of the hill and into the Shetani

Tsavo cheetah

Cave – bring a torch and walk with care. You can also scramble up the brittle, black slope to the rim of the Chaimu Crater, formed by another lava fountain. Always be alert for wild animals when exploring any of Tsavo's volcanic ruins.

The park's star attraction is the lush oasis of **Mzima Springs**. Rain falling in the Chyulu Hills is purified as it soaks through porous volcanic ash, and runs underground for 50km (31 miles) to resurface in two crystal-clear pools at Mzima. Walk along the path through the palm trees and reeds lining the banks of the pools, home to crocodiles and hippos, and stop at the viewing tank submerged in the upper pool for a fish-eye's view of barbels and mud suckers. Vervet and Sykes monkeys dot the fig trees.

Three rivers – the Galana, Athi and Tsavo – flow through the park, attracting large concentrations of game. But the denser growth of vegetation after a period of rain can make it very difficult to see the animals. Rain also brings out that scourge of Tsavo, the tsetse fly. This variety does not carry sleeping sickness, like those in the Congo, but it has a nasty sting and will sometimes swarm in the open windows and roofs of safari vehicles when driving through a thicket. A blast of insect spray is the best way to rid your vehicle of these invaders (who are also said to be attracted to the colour blue).

The park has two lodges – Kilaguni Serena Safari Lodge and Ngulia Safari Lodge – and a number of luxury tented camps including Finch Hattons, Severin Safari Camp and Ngulia Safari Camp. The park is on a bird migration corridor, and ornithologists gather here to study the migration patterns of the many species. Both lodges have waterholes to attract wildlife.

Tsavo East

Tsavo East, the larger of the two parks, is flatter, drier and less frequently visited. Voi Safari Lodge is built into the side of a hill with a fantastic vista across the sweeping plain. It, too, has a floodlit waterhole with a photography hide alongside. There are a number of small tented camps, including Satao Camp in the southern part of the park, Satao Rock Camp just outside on the border and Galdessa on the banks of the Galana River.

A distinguishing feature of Tsavo East is the stunning backdrop of the **Yatta Plateau**, one of the longest lava flows in the world. On the southern side of the plateau, the Tsavo and Athi Rivers join to form the Galana River just above Lugard's Falls, a series of rapids in a deep gorge cut into the bedrock by thousands of years of flowing water. Mudanda Rock is a popular haunt for leopard and makes for excellent photo opportunities, as does Aruba Dam, which attracts abundant game in the dry season. There are numerous security patrols throughout the park.

The Man-Eaters of Tsavo

While the railway was being built across the Tsavo plains at the beginning of the 20th century, a group of elderly male lions developed a taste for the workforce, eating 28 of the Indians and an uncounted number of Africans. Further up the line, at Kima, one European sleeping in a tent was dragged out and eaten. Somehow, the animals avoided every trap and after a while one was even confident enough to board the train and drag off its victims. The terror lasted 10 months until the man-eaters were ambushed and shot. Thereafter, the country on both sides of the track was left as a wildlife reserve, later to become Tsavo East and West National Parks.

THE COAST

This section covers Kenya's coast, including the island city of Mombasa, the beautiful beaches to the north and south, spectacular coral reefs and fascinating spots with an Arabic flavour, such as Malindi and the UNESCO-protected island of Lamu.

Mombasa

The city of **Mombasa** is the crossroads of Africa and Asia, and Kenya's oldest town. Its status as a port and trading centre is no less important now that tea and tourism have replaced gold and ivory as chief commodities.

Mombasa's origins may stretch back to 500BC, when Phoenician sailors put in at a coastal port that would correspond to Mombasa Island. The Greeks noted its trading potential in the 1st century AD, and later dhows, carried by the northeast

Diani Beach

monsoon from the Persian Gulf across the Indian Ocean, sailed along East Africa's coastal reef and found a navigable opening here. It was a magnet for Arabs, Persians, Turks, Indians, Portuguese and the British, all of whom left their mark.

In the 7th century, enterprising merchants from Persia and Arabia began to settle in the 'Land of the Zanj'

'Elephant' tusks on Moi Avenue

(Land of Black People), bringing with them the Islamic faith. Over the next 300 years, the intermingling of races and religions produced the Afro-Arab language and culture of Swahili.

Mombasa basked in wealth and power until the end of the 15th century, when the Portuguese arrived to plunder the coast. It took nearly 100 years of repeated assaults before the island stronghold fell, but that century of siege destroyed medieval Mombasa. The town you see today is essentially 19th century, except for the remains of Fort Jesus, built by the Portuguese for their garrison in 1593. They in turn were driven out in 1730, and a period of unrest followed in which Mombasa was ruled by the feuding Omani families who had aided the rebellion against the Portuguese. In the late 19th century, as a British protectorate, the town flourished once again.

Sightseeing in Mombasa can be covered in a day and is best done as early in the morning as possible, before your enthusiasm sinks into the torpor of the midday heat. The one monument you won't miss is the double arch across Moi Avenue formed by four huge, white, sheet-metal tusks, erected in 1952 to commemorate the visit of Queen Elizabeth. The tourist information office sits just beyond the 'elephant' tusks.

Fort Jesus, on the edge of the Old Town, is a good place to begin. Strategically placed at the southern entrance to Mombasa harbour, it stands on a coral ridge and has ramparts several metres thick. The grounds include a barracks, chapel, water cistern and well, guard rooms, gunpowder storeroom and an Omani house filled with artefacts from the Arab period.

The Old Town, just north of Fort Jesus, is the most fascinating part of Mombasa. Along the main thoroughfare of Ndia Kuu Road you can see some of the city's finest Arab buildings with carved doors and delicate wooden balconies. The narrow streets contain many of Mombasa's 49 mosques, the oldest of which, on Bachawy Road, is the Mandhry, built in 1570.

Lovely Hindu temples can also be found throughout the city. Among the most striking are the Swaminarayan Temple on Haile Selassie Avenue, the Jain Temple off Digo Road, and the Lord Shiva Temple on the edge of the old town.

The ruins of Mombasa's Fort Jesus

Gone are the days when tourists were welcomed aboard to join the haggling at the old dhow harbour. If you are lucky, you can watch the loading or unloading of the last of the dhows that still ply between Mombasa and the Gulf, their large lateen sails now supplemented by a motor.

You can wisely ignore the glut of curio shops near the Fort Jesus car park, as they are largely overpriced. A more authentic atmosphere for browsing can be found at the **Municipal Market**, still known by its colonial name, Mackinnon's Market. The adjacent Biashara Street is an excellent place to browse and shop for bright-coloured kangas and fabrics.

The South Coast

The Likoni Ferry links Mombasa to the south coast. Here you'll find that idyllic palm-fringed beach with soft, white sand of your dreams. Protected by a coral reef, the water offshore is warm and clear; surprisingly, the beaches here are quieter than most of the north coast's resort areas.

The best of the beaches is **Diani**, the major landmark of which is a 500-year-old baobab tree measuring 21m (71ft) in circumference, protected by presidential decree. Once you have seen the baobab, there is blissfully little to do but watch the sun rise and set, an often spectacular event.

There are plenty of watersports on offer all along the coast. Highly recommended is an excursion to **Wasini Island** and **Kisite-Mpunguti Marine National Park**. You will be collected from your hotel early in the morning for the hour's drive south to Shimoni, where a converted dhow takes you past coral islands to Kisite. The reef here offers some of the best snorkelling on the coast, but you can also gasp at the amazing corals and tropical fish by looking through glass-bottomed viewers from a small boat.

Following a gigantic seafood lunch at the **Charlie Claw's Island Restaurant**, you are entirely free to relax in the gar-

A dhow trip to Wasini Island – a highlight of the coast

dens or explore the island's early 19th-century Muslim village. On its edge are the stunning coral gardens. These surreal, honeycombed sculptures, spread over nearly 1ha (some 2.5 acres), were chiselled out by the fluctuating tides over the past 200 years. They remain, naturally, a work in progress.

If you want to give your suntan a rest, you can go inland to the game reserve at **Shimba Hills National Reserve**. The pleasant, wooded plateau rises to 450m (1,475ft), giving a refreshing change from the oppressive heat of the coast. Go early in the morning for the best chance to see the splendid sable antelopes with their scimitar-shaped horns, rare in Kenya. The males have magnificent coats of reddish-black, while the females are a lovely chestnut-brown colour. There are no lions, so it is safe for the antelopes and you to walk on the higher slopes – but look out for the odd python. You can stay overnight at the Shimba Forest Lodge, a spectacular tree lodge overlooking a water hole, noted for night-time game viewing.

The North Coast

The north coast is where Mombasa's elite have their homes, palatial residences shrouded in hibiscus and bougainvillea. This stretch of the coast is peppered with luxury hotels too.

There are, however, several attractions to divert you from the sun and sea. **Mamba Village** is the largest crocodile farm in Africa. You can walk along a shady pathway to observe some of its 10,000 reptiles basking in a series of breeding pools reclaimed from an old limestone quarry. Five o'clock is feeding time, when you can watch the crocs jump as high as 2m (6.5ft) out of the water for their dinner. There are also lovely botanical gardens, an aquarium with live corals, camel and horseback rides and a restaurant.

The Swiss agronomist Réné Haller was awarded a UN environmental protection prize for his success in converting the wasteland of a stone quarry into **Haller Park** (formerly Bamburi Nature Trail). This small forest harbours serval cats, monitor lizards, owls and other wildlife, including a pair of hippos in the central lake and giraffes.

North to Malindi

There are two sets of Arab ruins as you head north to Malindi. The first is at **Jumba La Mtwana** (Home of the Slave Master) outside Mtwapa, a 14th-century Swahili town whose ruined coral houses and mosques stretch down to the sea.

On the main Kilifi/Malindi road is the **Arabuko-Sokoke Forest Reserve**, home to rare mammals including the the fruit-eating Sokoke forest cat and the Sokoke golden-rumped elephant shrew. There are various common and rare birds found here, including the Sokoke scops owl. Visitors can enter the reserve on a number of access roads. There is a Visitors' Centre from where you can walk along the nature trail.

More substantial is the ancient town of **Gedi**, founded in the late 13th or early 14th century. The ruins here are extensive and well preserved; you can seek out the old mosques with their deep wells along eerie trails through the jungle, or pick your way among the walls of the palace, houses and pillar tombs. Rooms such as the 'House of the Scissors' and 'House of the Venetian Bead' indicate where Gedi's most interesting finds were made, many of which can be seen in the small museum. Next door to Gedi is the **Kipepeo Butterfly Farm** with a delightful Butterfly House.

Marine park

Just outside Gedi is the Watamu Marine National Park. Like its neighbour, Malindi Marine National Park, it is a protected area of white, coral sand beaches and clear, deep-blue lagoons where it is forbidden to fish or collect coral and seashells. An afternoon sundowner dhow trip into Mida Creek offers a chance for birdwatching along the edges of the mangroves and mudflats. Trips in glass-bottomed boats out to the coral reefs will be available from any of the hotels at Watamu or Malindi.

Malindi

If you've had a hard year and just want to bask for a week or two in the sun, then **Malindi** may be the place for you. Visitors are well catered for in this old Swahili town, which now relies solely on tourism for its prosperity. There is some excellent fishing and a pleasant market to browse through for souvenirs. However, it's usually too hot to move around, so you don't have to feel guilty about relaxing by the pool until you fly home.

There was a time when Malindi was more lively. With an eye to the main chance, the Sheikh of Malindi welcomed Vasco da Gama on that 1498 journey, giving him provisions for his voyage to India. His hospitality paid off with some golden years of trade with Portugal during the 16th century, until the rival state of Mombasa was conquered *(see page 13)* and the Portuguese transferred the

Feeding the fish in Malindi Marine Park

sheikh there. Malindi then sank back into the torpor you'll encounter today.

There's a monument to that brief moment of glory, out along the cliffs on the promontory, at the southern end of the Malindi harbour. The brilliant white Vasco da Gama pillar, engraved with Portugal's coat of arms, was erected by the explorer in gratitude to the sheikh for his warm reception. It has survived the ravages of the Turks, Arabs and British and is one of the very few authentic Portuguese relics left on the coast.

Lamu

For an idea of what Malindi or Mombasa looked like when the Arabs ruled the coast, make the trip to the island of **Lamu**, a backwater of Swahili culture off Kenya's northern shore. Its origins date to the 2nd century and along with Manda and Pate it was one of the most prosperous commercial centres of the archipelago until its decline in the late 1800s. Unlike its neighbours, Lamu survived, remaining isolated from modern technology and the Western world until shipping and the wave of tourism brought a resurgence to its economy in the 1960s.

It is best reached by small aircraft on one of the regular, inexpensive flights from Nairobi, Malindi or Mombasa, as the overland route is rough and often flooded. You'll be welcomed at the airstrip on Manda Island by an eager gang of locals ready to carry your bags to the ferry for the short crossing to Lamu.

Your first few hours in Lamu may prove something of a cultural shock. There are no cars here; the main mode of transport is donkeys and they and their droppings are everywhere. Open sewers run alongside the narrow streets, and refuse is often dumped into the sea. But you soon forget the unsanitary sights and smells as you fall into the languid rhythm of this town.

Arabic architecture

The traditional Islamic community has made few concessions to the modern world. Women, especially, should be dressed in a conservative manner to avoid causing offence, though you'll feel pretty conspicuous in shorts when everyone else is swathed in black from head to toe. Be extra sensitive about photographs here; always ask before you point your camera at someone.

Lamu's stone houses are the best legacy of Swahili architecture. These plain, thick, coral walls often conceal elaborate interior ornamentation of carved plasterwork and wall niches. You can see a fine example, restored to portray the early way of life, at the **Swahili House Museum**.

The most beautiful feature of Lamu's houses is their carved wooden doors. Some date to the 18th century, but even the most modern retain the style, forms and craftsmanship of centuries-old traditions. There are excellent specimens on display at the

Woman in Lamu

Lamu Museum. One of the finest small museums in Kenya, it offers explanations of Lamu's architecture and insights into the traditions of this complex culture. The pride of the museum are two magnificent *siwas* (ceremonial horns), one of carved ivory 2m (6.5ft) long and the other, slightly shorter, of brass.

You can eat seafood for a song at the small restaurants along the waterfront, but only three places on the island sell alcohol. The first is Petley's Inn, a landmark meeting place for locals and travellers alike. The second is the Peponi Hotel *(see page 138)*, 3km (2 miles) down the road at Shela. This is Lamu's swimming beach, easily reached by dhow if you don't want to walk. The third is Diamond Beach Village on Manda Island.

There are plenty of local boatmen to take you fishing or sailing on a dhow around the other islands. But the best way to spend your days in Lamu is to wander through its back streets, or simply sit on a rooftop or in the main square by the old fort, watching the world go by.

WHAT TO DO

SPORTS

Kenya offers wide opportunities for sports and outdoor recreation year-round due to its excellent climate. Watersports, hiking, fishing, climbing, tennis and riding are popular.

Watersports

Watersports of all types are prolific throughout Kenya. You will find the coastal waters delightfully warm for swimming, with none of the health risks or crocodiles of the inland rivers and lakes. The sharks stay outside the reef.

If you've never gone snorkelling before, Kenya's amazing coral reefs provide excellent opportunities. There are glass-bottomed boats that will take you out to the shallow reefs for hire at hotels and on the beaches; many of these boats have snorkelling gear on board. Wear rubber-soled shoes to protect your feet from the razor-sharp coral. Scuba-diving equipment can also be hired, and many hotels offer diving tuition.

Some beach resorts offer waterskiing, windsurfing and kite surfing. You can, in theory, waterski on some of the inland lakes (Lake Naivasha, Lake Baringo and Victoria), but the possibility of contracting bilharzia makes it a risky business; best to stick to the coast. Sailing is a great way to enjoy the inland waterways, the best spots being

Giriama dancer, Mombasa

When to go

The best time of year to explore the marine world is October to March, when the northeast monsoon (*kaskazi*) blows. From April to September, the south-east kusi brings cooler conditions, rougher waters and high winds – though the water temperature never drops below 24°C (75°F).

Learning to dive

Lake Naivasha and Lake Victoria. If you're visiting Lamu, a dhow trip around the nearby islands is a timeless thrill. Canoeing and white-water rafting are also growing sports, and river trips can be arranged at some lodges and hotel resorts.

Deep-sea fishing can also be arranged on the spot through hotels along the coast. River and lake fishing can be booked through specialist travel agents.

Hiking and Climbing

Kenya's spectacular mountains and scenic hills make hiking a great lure. Some of the most accessible regions for walking include Mount Kenya, the Aberdare Mountains, the Chyulu Hills, Hell's Gate, and Mounts Susua and Longonot and the Menengai Crater in the Rift Valley. Ramblers in the Ngong Hills, southwest of Nairobi, should have a security guard. Further afield, Ololokwe Mountain just north of Samburu, the Cherangani Hills and Mount Elgon are considered superb walking country. Before setting off, pick up a good guidebook and detailed map of the region you plan to visit.

Experienced and fearless mountain climbers can attempt an ascent to the higher peaks of Mount Kenya. Climbs are organised by the Nairobi-based Mountain Club of Kenya or through your travel agent and begin at the Naro Moru River Lodge, which hires out porters and equipment. A reasonably fit novice can climb the lower peak, Lenana, in a couple of days.

Other Sports

Tennis and other racket sports are on offer at many of the larger hotels and sports clubs. Fitness centres and health spas can be found at a number of hotels and lodges around the country.

Riding, an imperial legacy, is most popular in the Highlands. A good place to enquire about hiring horses is the Karen shopping centre outside Nairobi. Pony trekking and mountain biking through the Rift Valley or elsewhere can often be arranged through your lodge or hotel. Horse-racing has been a popu-

Hot-Air Ballooning

Not for the light of pocket, nor for anyone adverse to extremely early mornings (a 5.30am start is typical), balloon safaris nonetheless offer a truly unique opportunity for game-spotting. They are particularly popular over the Maasai Mara, whose wide, open plains allow excellent visibility, and can be booked from the UK (through your tour operator) or on arrival in Kenya. You'll spend an hour or so drifting above the animals, before landing and being served a champagne breakfast out in the bush. Although these rides are expensive (around £200), most people claim that they are money well spent. But for those whose budget doesn't quite stretch to it, even just watching the balloons drift over the plains at sunrise is impressive. One tip: take a hat to protect your head from the heat of the burner.

lar sport in Kenya since the early 20th century, though the only racetrack to hold regular meetings is the Ngong Race Course on the outskirts of Nairobi. The season runs from September to July, when meetings are held most Sunday afternoons.

Golf is also popular, with hotels and country clubs across Kenya geared towards catering to the golfer's every whim.

SHOPPING

The big challenge in shopping for souvenirs of your stay in Kenya is sorting out genuine artworks from mass-produced junk. The first rule of thumb is to avoid any shop with a sign that offers 'curios'. These may well be handcarved on an assembly line, without the careful craftsmanship of the real thing.

Two good places in Nairobi to find authentic, quality African crafts are Utamaduni, off Langata Road (a percentage is donated to wildlife conservation) and African Heritage, with showrooms on the Mombasa Highway and at Carnivore restaurant. You can find cheaper goods at the city market, but you'll have to bargain hard. Crafts co-operatives representing rural artisans have retail shops in the towns, and you can often visit textile, bead and woodcarving workshops on the outskirts. Visit the colourful open-air 'Maasai Markets' around Nairobi – at the Globe Roundabout on Tuesdays, Village Market on Fridays and at Yaya Centre on Sundays. If you can't make the major market days, the Triangle Market in Westlands is open seven days a week. For more quality souvenirs, visit the Banana Box at the Sarit Centre, Blue Rhino at ABC Place, and Collector's Den at the Hilton Hotel.

Bargain hunt

Bargaining is very much a part of life in East Africa. Seasoned shoppers advise that you start your bargaining at half the suggested price. If prices are marked, there is probably less room for negotiation.

Traditional artefacts for sale in Mombasa

In Mombasa look out for antiques: Arab brasswork, trays and Zanzibar chests, although antique chests are harder to find now. The coast is also a good place to buy colourful fabrics – *kikois* for men, *kangas* and *kitenges* for women – which can be worn as beach wraps or used for bedspreads and tablecloths.

Note that animal skins or products bought without government permits – and you won't get one – are strictly illegal, as are game trophies and ivory products. Coral and seashells will probably have been plundered from one of the protected marine parks, so their purchase is also highly illegal.

ENTERTAINMENT

The big hotels in Nairobi, Mombasa and on the coast should be able to satisfy an urge for clubbing. You'll often be entertained by bands performing American and European pop music. Traditional African music can be difficult to track

African handicrafts

down. Native dancing is often performed at lodges and hotels, but it can bear the same relationship to the real thing as the curios in souvenir shops do to authentic African art.

A more genuine display of African dancing is available at the Bomas of Kenya, near Nairobi National Park, where you can see spectacular Samburu war dances, Kamba acrobatics, a Giriama wedding dance and an expurgated version of the Kikuyu circumcision ceremony that is still carried on by men though suppressed by women.

The publications *Going Out Guide* and *Go Places* list current exhibitions and cultural events in the capital. Nairobi's Gallery Watatu, Rahimtulla Museum of Modern Art (RaMoMa) on Upper Hill and a number of art galleries in the upmarket shopping centres display contemporary African art.

CHILDREN

There are pros and cons of taking children on safari. There is lots to see, traditional accommodation offers a unique experience, and animal-loving children will be in their element. Babysitting *(see page 107)* is usually available in hotels and camps at a reasonable price. Most upmarket hotels and lodges have pools. However, most safaris involve long, bumpy journeys and some very early morning starts. Some safaris are not available to children under the age of 12.

Festivals and Events

Check <www.kenyabuzz.com> or the daily newspapers for weekly sporting, cultural and social event updates.

January Fishing competitions in Mtwapa and Kilifi. Hog Charge (bicycle cross-country fundraiser for Rhino Ark). Autocross/quattro cross events.
February 10 to 4 mountain bike challenge, Mount Kenya. Kijani Trust musical events. FEI Show Jumping Gauntlet, Jamhuri Park, Nairobi. Fishing competitions in Kilifi, Watamu and Malindi.
March KCB Safari Rally, autocross, quattro cross. Kijani Trust musical events. FEI Show Jumping Challenge, Jamhuri Park, Nairobi. Fishing competitions in Mtwapa, Watamu and Mombasa.
April KCB Rally, Cross Country Rally Challenge. Easter Frolic, Kilifi/Mtwapa. Easter Show (equestrian events), Jamhuri Park. Naivasha Fun Weekend (equestrian events), Sanctuary Farm.
May Mombasa Marathon. KCB Rally, Western Kenya. Rhino Charge (off-road endurance event). Anti Stock Theft Unit Horse Show, Gilgil.
June Safaricom Lewa Marathon. Tusker Safari Rugby Sevens. National Barista Championships. Agricultural Society of Kenya Nakuru Show.
July KCB Rally. Maralal International Camel Derby. National Cricket League (until September).
August Laikipia International Camel Derby. Mombasa International Show.
September Schweppes Concours d'Elegance. Horse racing season starts at Ngong Racecourse. Agricultural Society of Kenya Nairobi Show.
October KCB Guru Nanak Rally. Malindi International Fishing Festival. East African Kennel Club Dog Show, Nairobi. Driftwood Rugby Sevens, <www.kenyarfu.com>. Malindi Fishing Festival.
November Annual Skydiving Boogie, Diani Beach. Motor Rally, Kisumu. East African Safari Classic Rally. Quattro Charge. Manyatta Polo Tournament, Gilgil. Fishing Competition in Mtwapa. Lamu Cultural Festival.
December Horse of the Year Show, Jamhuri Park. Uhuru Cup, Ngong Racecourse. Christmas craft fairs and pantomimes (see newspapers for dates). Boxing Day races at Ngong Racecourse.

EATING OUT

The variety of the cuisine in Kenya reflects the country's rich history. It was the Arabs who started the cosmopolitan trend in local cuisine here, sailing in with their dried fruits, rice and spices and expanding the diet of the coastal Swahilis. But it took centuries for this influence to spread inland, where people subsisted on a diet heavy in sorghum and millet, supplemented only by whatever fruits, roots and seeds they could find.

The arrival of the Portuguese in 1498 changed all that, with the introduction of foods from newly discovered Brazil. Maize, bananas, pineapples, chillies, peppers, sweet potatoes and manioc were all brought into East Africa, where most of them were destined to become local staples. The Portuguese

The Carnivore restaurant is a Nairobi institution

also brought lemons, limes and oranges from China and India, as well as introducing domestic pigs.

The British were next to influence eating and drinking habits in Kenya, importing new breeds of sheep, goats and cattle, together with luxuries such as strawberries and asparagus. They planted high-quality coffee and taught their cooks how to make lumpy custard, as well as which way to serve the port with up-country 'Njoro Stilton'.

They also imported thousands of Indians to build the railway to Uganda, and with

Coconut palm

The coconut palm provides food, drink, cooking oil, fibre for rope and matting, and leaves for thatching.

these immigrants came the curries, chapatis and chutneys that are now as traditional a Sunday lunch in Kenya as roast beef is in Yorkshire. Later, between and after the wars, the Europeans arrived with their spicy sausages and pastas. More recently, global fast foods from hamburgers to pizzas have appeared in Nairobi.

In the 40 or so years since Kenya gained its independence from Britain the cuisine has been transformed by the influence of innumerable and varied cooking styles, from Ethiopian, Indian and Thai to French and Italian. The result is an incredible variety of high-quality food, usually at very reasonable prices.

Quantities are enormous and cheese and desserts are an honourable supplement to the meal, alongside the delicious,

Fresh produce by the basketful

ripe pineapples, pawpaws and mangoes. On safari, you will be glad of the traditional English breakfasts usually served to satisfy appetites after a dawn game drive.

One of the great treats of Kenya is the wonderful fresh seafood served on the coast: large lobsters, superb shrimp and prawns, all astoundingly cheap compared with European or American prices – and excellent kingfish and swordfish. If you order them simply grilled, with at most a butter sauce, you will have tasted one of Kenya's best meals.

Vegetarians are well catered for at the hotels and lodges. In the cities and on the coast, there are many fine Indian, Italian and Chinese restaurants. Some excellent pizzas can also be found on the north coast in Malindi. African food can best be sampled at the African barbecues put on weekly by many hotels and lodges.

The buffet service, favoured by most hotels for at least one of their daily meals, gives you as generous portions as you could wish. In Kenya, to eat well without spending a fortune, go for the buffet spreads and seafood.

Eating out is one of the great pleasures of Kenya. There are plenty of excellent restaurants in Nairobi and, at most of them, you'd be hard pressed to spend much more than 1,000 shillings (£8–10) per person excluding wine, although at a few of the really expensive places you could pay three times as much, with appetisers and dessert.

If you're after a quick snack, a number of Nairobi's shopping centres (Sarit, Yaya, ABC Place, Village Market, The Junction) have a selection of restaurants or food courts offering local dishes, salad bars, Italian, European, Indian and fast foods.

Local Cuisine

Traditionally, Kenyans breakfast on *mandazi* (a triangular-shaped doughnut) washed down with sweet milky tea. Lunch is *ugali* (corn meal porridge) eaten with vegetable or meat stew. Dinner might be *nyama choma* (grilled meat, often goat) and the rural staple, *sukuma wiki*, which literally translates as 'getting through the week' and is a variation on spinach. *Irio*, a Kikuyu mixture of mashed potatoes and peas with maize kernels, is another dish to try, as is *kuku wakupaka*, a spiced chicken recipe from Lamu. Also look out for restaurants serving *nyama choma* (roast meat), which often consists of goat, chicken or beef. Meat is typically accompanied by clay pots filled with sweet potatoes, arrowroot, cassava and other varieties of root vegetables.

Though the national cuisine may seem a little bland to visitors with adventurous culinary tastes, the wide and delicious range of other foods on offer more than makes up for it. Fish-eaters can indulge in lobster, prawns, crayfish, Nile perch, tilapia (a freshwater fish similar to perch), parrot fish,

Fresh fish is abundant on the coast

or delicious smoked sailfish, the Kenyan equivalent to smoked salmon. Meat-eaters can eat their fill of zebra, gazelle, crocodile, giraffe, ostrich, or the rather more ordinary beef or Molo lamb. Healthy-eating enthusiasts can tuck into passion fruit, paw-paw, guavas, pineapple, plums, oranges, bananas and other fruits. To see and sample the wide range of fresh vegetables and fruit on offer, you should call into Nairobi's City Market, where foods from asparagus to tree tomato will be for sale.

And don't miss snacks such as warm toasted cashew nuts, macadamia nuts and coconuts, or avocados with Worcestershire sauce. Other snacks to try include plantain, arrowroot or cassava chips.

What to Drink
Wining can be very easily dealt with: drink the beer. Kenya's local brews – Tusker Malt Lager, White Cap and Pilsner –

are excellent and inexpensive, served cool or warm according to your preference. In hotels and restaurants all imported wines and spirits are fairly costly. As far as wine is concerned, attempts were made to grow wine-producing grapes near Naivasha, but were abandoned when South African and European wines began to flood the market. Imported wine in restaurants is expensive by Kenyan standards, but not excessively so for European or American visitors. Wine in supermarkets is reasonably priced, considering how far it has travelled.

For liqueurs, locally grown options include the coffee-flavoured Kenya Gold or Kenya Cane, a white rum made from sugar cane and similar to Bacardi.

The Tamarind

Even if dining is all 'packaged' in your hotel holiday, try to escape for just one meal out at the superb Tamarind, of which there are branches in both Nairobi and Mombasa. In Nairobi, the Tamarind has sea-blue decor and consistently superb food, and a visit here is more an evening out than a meal: start in the upstairs bar with 'nibbles' of tiny fried prawns, coconut strips and banana crisps. For a more substantial starter, try smoked trout with horseradish sauce, a mound of the minuscule Mombasa oysters, fish tartare or perhaps dried impala. For the main course, there are spiny lobsters, king crab claws, Malindi sole, or a mixture of the lot in a superb seafood casserole. Mombasa's Tamarind is Moorish-styled, set on a hill overlooking the city's old harbour, and has tables set out on the flower-filled terrace. The speciality of the house is also seafood: try lobster Tamarind, fish tartare, prawns piri piri and coupe bahari, or just order oysters and champagne and enjoy being alive. If you feel lucky, the Golden Key Casino is upstairs. Or, if you feel nautical, take the Tamarind Dhow and enjoy a romantic evening of seafood and light music while floating under the stars.

HANDY TRAVEL TIPS

An A–Z Summary of Practical Information

A

ACCOMMODATION

Kenya's tourist hotels are classified as Town Hotels, Vacation Hotels, Lodges and Tented Camps. In addition, there is self-catering accommodation. Most towns have rudimentary so-called 'boarding and lodgings', which offer little more than a bed, well water and minimal security; these are not recommended for tourists.

Hotels. Kenya's hotels vary enormously in price and facilities, and the one- to five-star rating given by the Ministry of Tourism is not an accurate basis of comparison. It's better to enquire at a local travel agent, or book through one of the larger hotel chains. Kenya's luxury hotels offer extremely high standards of service and are comparable to the best hotels anywhere in the world. First- and second-class hotels vary widely in service and facilities, but are generally comfortable with private bath and European-type food. Hotel prices are often discounted during the low season and there is usually a reduction for children under 12.

Lodges. Accommodation is limited in the national parks and reserves, so lodges must be booked well in advance, especially during high season. Food and facilities are generally of good to high standards.

Permanent tented camps. These permanently sited canvas tents are pitched on concrete bases or raised wooden platforms, usually situated with good views or in harmonious settings. Many offer a surprising degree of luxury and most a high standard of services, with flushable toilets, hot and cold running water and electricity.

Self-catering. Sturdily built, self-help bandas are available in many game parks. They offer cooking facilities, which vary considerably from a propane gas stove to a campfire; you will need to bring your own bedding, food and drink. These are popular with Kenyans during high season and public holidays, so book ahead. Bookings can be made through the KWS Tourism Department, tel: Nairobi +254 (0)20-600800 or 602345, <www.kws.go.ke>.

In towns, some of the larger hotels offer apartments or boarding houses for extended stays. Self-catering villas, apartments or cottages are becoming more widely available, especially on the coast. Check with a travel agent, or try contacting Exclusive Classic Properties, Village Market, tel: 020-7121074/7121099, <www.exclusive classicproperties.com>, or Langata Link, Langata South Road, tel: 020-890699/891333, <www.kenyasafarihomes.com>, which act as agents for many holiday homeowners.

AIRPORTS

Kenya is served by two international airports. Flight and airport information can be obtained at <www.kenyaairports.com>. The **Jomo Kenyatta International Airport** is 30 minutes' drive from Nairobi's city centre. Mombasa's **Moi International Airport** on the Kenya coast is closer to the town centre, but most of the tourist hotels are at various distances to the north or south of the town. Porters will take heavy bags to customs for you, and will assist you to bus stops and taxi stands for modest tips.

Most tourist hotels have their own minibuses at the airports to transport guests. A public bus serves both the Jomo Kenyatta and Moi airports. Numerous taxis are on hand, but establish the fare first.

Departure. Airport tax is included in the cost of your ticket. Duty-free purchases can only be made in foreign or Kenya currency. Check your baggage allowance with your airline and do not exceed it, as overweight charges can run into 500Ksh per kilo.

Internal air travel. Domestic flights are a convenient and affordable means of travel. Kenya Airways and Fly540.com have regular flights to Mombasa and Malindi. Frequent scheduled flights with Air Kenya (<www.airkenya.com>) and Safarilink (<www.safarilink.co.ke>) and charter flights operate from Nairobi's Wilson Airport and from Mombasa and Malindi to the main towns and game parks.

B

BABYSITTERS

Most hotels will arrange babysitting services. Rates vary depending on location and on the number of children, but are never excessive.

BUDGETING FOR YOUR TRIP

The following list will give you some idea of what to expect in Kenya; however, these prices are approximate, so add a small contingency figure to allow for inflation. The Kenya shilling and exchange rate fluctuates widely, and most tour operators and hotels quote their rates in US dollars. Otherwise, prices are given here in the local currency.

Accommodation. Rates for double room, high season: Luxury hotels US$200–400 (full board); town hotels US$65–250 (bed and breakfast); beach hotels US$150–300 (half board); lodges US$200–400 (full board); permanent tented camps US$200–450 (full board).

Attractions. Museums/historic ruins 500–1,200Ksh (see <www.museums.or.ke>); visits to tribal villages 600–1,200Ksh; boat trips 1,700–4,000Ksh per hour.

Babysitters. 300–500Ksh per day plus transport.

Camping. In national parks and reserves 700–1,000Ksh per night per person with own tent; booking is usually done on arrival. Private campsites 250–300Ksh per night.

Car hire. International firms, all inclusive rates. Toyota 110 (4 seats): 5,000–8,000Ksh per day; 47,000Ksh per week. Suzuki Vitara (small 4WD): 12,000Ksh per day; 80,000Ksh per week. Mitsubishi Pajero (large 4WD): 16,000Ksh per day; 115,000Ksh per week. (Rates include unlimited mileage and insurance. Petrol: 85Ksh per litre.)

Domestic flights. Nairobi–Mombasa (one way) 4,750Ksh; Nairobi–Maasai Mara US$200 (return); Mombasa–Lamu US$150 (return); Malindi–Lamu US$105 (return). All are scheduled flights.

Game park entrance fees. US$20–40 adults, 300–800Ksh vehicles per day. Further information can be obtained from Kenya Wildlife Service (KWS), <www.kws.go.ke>. Proposed fee increases from May 2008: US$40–60 adults, 300–1,000Ksh vehicles per day.

Meals and Drinks. Breakfast from 250Ksh; lunch 450–1,000Ksh (one course); dinner 450–1,000Ksh (one course), 2,000-4,000Ksh (three-course meal in a good restaurant); mineral water 30–150Ksh (shops), 160–200Ksh (hotels); beer 60–250Ksh; wine 140–300Ksh per glass, from 675Ksh per bottle.

C

CAMPING

Some people would say camping is the only way to experience the real Kenya. It has become a thriving 'extra' for Kenya's tour operators, and the better-off visitor can experience the thrill of Kenya's vast skies and the endless bush at a comfortably fitted site. But for the enterprising visitor (and resident alike), camping in Kenya's wild bushlands can be an inexpensive and unforgettable experience.

Find a site well before sunset, for in tropical Africa it can be pitch dark half an hour after the sun starts to go down. Choose level ground with short grass and plenty of shade, but beware of the type of tree you camp under: thorn trees are good for shade and have no climbing leopards and snakes, but you'll usually find a thick carpet of thorns underneath them. Make sure the rear windows face the prevailing wind. Do not set camp on, or too near, a sandy expanse of a dry river-bed – a tropical rainstorm miles away can send un-bridled water gushing down towards you. Avoid camping right across or too near a game trail – you could find an animal stumbling into your guy ropes. In addition, there is always the danger of a fire going wild. Learn to build 'safe' fires and keep the flames under control at all times. If necessary, camping equipment can be hired in Nairobi.

CAR HIRE

To hire a car in Kenya you must be over 23 and under 70 years of age and possess a valid driver's licence from your country of residence, or an international driver's permit. The driver must have held the licence for a minimum period of two years at the time of hiring a vehicle.

All the major international car-hire firms are represented in Kenya and numerous local firms offer competitive rates. Prices are higher than in Europe and North America. A deposit and daily collision damage insurance are compulsory. Safety rather than price should be your first consideration in choosing a car-hire firm: a breakdown in a remote area or game park is more than an inconvenience – it can pose a real danger. Confirm in writing that if the car breaks down, the car-hire company will replace it with another vehicle. Always check the oil, water, tyres, and engine; determine the grade of petrol required and ensure that you have at least one good spare and the essential tools. If possible, hire the car the day before setting out on the road in order to drive around town and check the condition of the vehicle.

Although 4-wheel-drive vehicles are not essential, they are strongly advisable for driving in game parks and reserves.

CLIMATE

Since Kenya is on the equator, the climate remains pretty stable throughout the year. Days are sunny and hot, but nights can be cool. The weather is warm and dry from mid-December to mid-March, and the long rains fall between late March and May. July and August form the coldest season. September to October are the best times to visit, as the weather is good prior to the short rains that begin in late October through to mid-December. Coastal temperatures range from 28°C (82°F) to 32°C (90°F) with varying degrees of humidity.

CLOTHING

Lightweight, cotton casual wear is fine on safari, and a hat and sunglasses are recommended for protection against the strong sun. Bright colours are best avoided, as they can attract insects and make you too conspicuous in the bush. Evenings in Nairobi are cool, and can be very chilly in the Highlands. Warm clothing is necessary after sunset and in early mornings. At lower altitudes, a long-sleeved shirt and long trousers are a deterrent to mosquitoes. Trainers are the most versatile footwear – you may want to bring hiking boots if you plan to do a lot of walking in the bush, and waterproof shoes in the rainy seasons.

Jacket and tie are needed only in the classiest restaurants. Nudity and topless sunbathing on beaches or in public places are forbidden.

CRIME AND SAFETY

Some areas in Nairobi and Mombasa are best avoided after dark; take a taxi directly to your destination. Avoid cutting through parks at night or walking alone on empty highways, lanes or on beaches at night.

Do not carry large sums of cash or travellers' cheques with you. Lock all articles in the boot of your car, and lock the car too. When driving through towns and cities, remember to keep your windows up and the doors locked – there are tricksters who will try to snatch jewellery and other such valuables from you or your car, or make you believe you have a puncture. Drive to the nearest petrol station if you are at all concerned. Do not leave valuable personal belongings unattended on beaches and in public places, and be careful of pickpockets.

For those travelling up-country or to remote areas on their own, note the possibility of attacks by armed bandits *(shiftas)* in certain areas. Police stations and army posts along the route will have current information on the area and will arrange guarded convoys if necessary. Do not accept sweets or other food from strangers, as it may be drugged. The Tourist Help Line offers a 24-hour service for security, road and weather information, tel: 020-604767/605485/ 0722-745645/0733-617499, email: <safetour@wananchi.com>.

CUSTOMS AND ENTRY FORMALITIES

Everyone entering Kenya is required to have a visa. All nationals should apply for a visa from one of the embassies or consulates in their country, or purchase one at the airport or border crossing on arrival. If buying one on arrival, ensure you have sufficient cash on you: a single-entry visa, valid for three months, costs US$50 (payable in dollars, euros or sterling); a multiple-entry visa is US$100; a transit visa is US$20. Make sure that your passport is valid for at least six months beyond the proposed end of your stay. Consult your travel agent or <www.kenya-airways.com> for a visa application form.

Currency. You can bring any amount of foreign currency into Kenya and take it out again when you leave. However, exporting of Kenyan currency is not recommended, since it will be difficult to exchange outside the country.

D

DISABLED TRAVELLERS

Kenyans generally have a helpful attitude towards disabled travellers. Most of the larger hotels in town and on the coast have lifts. Traffic is a bigger problem; be careful crossing the busy streets. In the game parks, negotiating narrow stone paths at some of the lodges may be difficult in a wheelchair. Seek advice from a knowledgeable travel agent when choosing a lodge. Also, the rough, bumpy roads may cause discomfort even in the most luxurious safari vehicle.

DRIVING

Driving in many parts of Kenya is at best a challenge and at worst a nightmare. You may want to leave much of the driving, especially on the unpaved dirt tracks, to experienced, well-trained tour drivers.

Driving conditions. Kenyan motorists drive on the left and overtake on the right. Most vehicles have the steering wheel on the right. Roads are narrow, so ensure you have full view of the stretch ahead before attempting to overtake. Road conditions in many places are appalling: even parts of the main Nairobi–Mombasa–Nakuru highway can have unexpected potholes. Roads throughout the country are now being upgraded and resurfaced so conditions are varied at any given time. Drive slowly on rough roads to maintain control of your vehicle. Be prepared for unexpected manoeuvres and poor driving standards.

Dirt roads quickly turn to mud when it rains. When approaching a nasty-looking patch of mud or water, it's best to check the depth first if possible; if not, keep moving in second gear until you're clear.

Driving in the National Parks. Speeds are strictly limited to 40kph (25mph) and sometimes less, so as not to frighten the wild animals. For the same reason, avoid all loud noises and brusque movements.

Distances. Here are some approximate road distances in km (miles):

Nairobi–Eldoret	310 (190)	Mombasa–Eldoret	800 (495)
Nairobi–Kisumu	350 (215)	Mombasa–Kisumu	845 (525)
Nairobi–Malindi	615 (380)	Mombasa–Malindi	120 (75)
Nairobi–Mombasa	490 (305)	Mombasa–Marsabit	1,110 (690)
Nairobi–Nanyuki	200 (125)	Mombasa–Moyale	1,380 (855)
Nairobi–Nyeri	160 (100)	Mombasa–Nakuru	650 (405)

Traffic police. Make sure your hire car has the proper insurance and PSV (passenger service vehicle) licence stickers in case you are pulled over. For minor traffic offences, the police impose fines on the spot. You will have to appear in court and pay the fine in cash.

Breakdowns. Before setting out for long-distance driving, contact the Automobile Association of Kenya (<www.aakenya.co.ke>), the headquarters of which are in Nairobi. The AA will advise on the road conditions ahead, and on how to obtain help in an emergency. When travelling off the main routes, consider taking jerry cans of petrol and water. If you do have a breakdown, spare parts and proper tools may be scarce. Agree a price with local mechanics before any work begins.

AA telephones. Nairobi: 020-825060/1/2/3 or 020-2723195; Mombasa: 041-2492431; Malindi: 042-21009; Eldoret: 053-2030623; Kisumu 057-2021940; Nyeri: 061-2032372; Meru: 064-32896; Kisii 058-21429; Nakuru: 051-2217293; Nanyuki: 062-32677.

E

ELECTRICITY

Major towns and cities are supplied with 240 volts, 50 cycles AC. Some lodges have independent power generators, which vary in voltage. Kenyan plugs are of the three square-pin 13-amp type.

EMBASSIES, CONSULATES AND HIGH COMMISSIONS

Australia: High Commission: Riverside Drive, PO Box 39341, Nairobi; tel: 020-4445034/4445039/3752620.
Canada: High Commission: Limuru Road, Gigiri, PO Box 1013, 00621 Nairobi; tel: 020-3663000.
Ireland: Consulate: Owashika Road, off Isaac Githanju Road, PO Box 30659, 00100 Nairobi; tel: 020-3878043/3871635.
New Zealand: Contact the Kenyan local authorities or the UK High Commission.
South Africa: Embassy: Lenana Road, Kilimani, PO Box 42441, 00100 Nairobi; tel: 020-2827100, email: <sahc@africaonline.co.ke>.
UK: High Commission: Upper Hill Road, PO Box 30465, Nairobi; tel: 020-2844000; <www.britishhighcommission.gov.uk/kenya>.
US: Embassy: Embassy Building, United Nations Avenue, Gigiri, PO Box 30137, Nairobi; tel: 020-3636000.

EMERGENCIES

Police, Fire, Ambulance anywhere in Kenya, tel: 999.
Police Headquarters, Nairobi area, tel: 020-240000.
Police Headquarters, Mombasa, tel: 041-222121.
St John's Ambulance, Nairobi, tel: 020-210000.
Tourist Help Line, tel: 020-604767/605485 or 0722-745645 or
0733-617499, email: <safetour@wananchi.com>.

G

GETTING TO KENYA

From the UK by air. Kenya Airways and British Airways have
daily, direct flights from London (Heathrow) to Nairobi (some
flights are direct to Mombasa), stopping at different places en route
depending on day of travel. Passengers from Ireland and the
provinces must connect at London.

Package tours from the UK. A comprehensive range of tours is available, from full board in a top-class hotel including safaris, to budget
accommodation with optional excursions and even a growing number of ecologically friendly vacations. Safaris are often organised for
groups with special interests. For the independent traveller, it is often
possible to purchase flight-only tickets on these charter flights.

From North America by air. Nairobi is serviced by direct flights via
London or other European cities from several North American cities
on any day of the week. Connections can be made daily from many
North American cities.

Package tours from the US. A variety of Group Inclusive Tours (GIT),
usually of three weeks' duration, combine visits to cities such as
Capetown, Cairo and Casablanca with wildlife tours of Kenya. Several programmes include Brazil as the first stopover point. From there,

travel is due east to South Africa and then north to Victoria Falls, Kenya, and Tanzania or Uganda. Included in the cost of the tour are roundtrip air transport transfers, accommodation at de luxe hotels and lodges, all or most meals, tips, and the services of a guide. A 15-day OTC (One-Stop Inclusive Tour Charter) has been designed for travellers who want to visit only Kenya and spend nine days on safari.

L

LANGUAGE

Swahili, the lingua franca of East Africa, was originally written in Arabic characters. When British missionaries introduced the Latin alphabet, they adopted as phonetic a transliteration as possible, so that Swahili is rather easy to pronounce. More than 40 tribal languages are spoken in Kenya. Most people, however, speak English remarkably well, and so English, whatever accent you have, will be understood, except well off the beaten track, where you'll need Swahili. *Berlitz Swahili Phrase Book & Dictionary* should help you get by.

Hello	**Jambo**
Good morning/evening	**Habari za asubuhi/jioni**
How are you?	**Habari**
Fine/Very well	**Nzuri/Nzuri sana**
Please/Thank you	**Tafadhali/Asante**
Goodbye/See you soon	**Kwaheri/Tutaonana**

LAUNDRY AND DRY CLEANING

Hotel, lodge and camp laundry is generally done well and not too expensive. If you are in central Nairobi, you may want to try one of the many fast-service dry-cleaners. Ask at the reception desk for the one nearest your hotel, as the in-house charges may be rather high. There are no self-service launderettes in Kenya.

M

MEDIA

Kenya has four well-established English-language daily **papers**, *The Nation*, *The Standard* and the *Kenya Times*, and their Sunday counterparts, and the weekly *East African*. The *International Express* and the *Weekly Telegraph* provide a compilation of the week's British news and major international events. There are a wide range of English-language monthly and quarterly **magazines** printed in Kenya, including the magazine *Travel News & Lifestyle East Africa* and *Swara*. Many international newspapers and magazines are sold on newspaper stands and in stationers' shops in the large hotels several days later, at a price.

Kenya has over seven **radio** stations broadcasting in FM (in English, Swahili or Kikuyu) with a number that can be picked up countrywide. Many stations broadcast from 6am to midnight, with news on the hour. In Nairobi, Mombasa and major up-country towns, KTN, KBC, Nation and Metro **TV** stations broadcast excerpts from CNN, Sky News and BBC news and local programming round the clock. Satellite television – DSTV – is available; many of its sports and news programmes are shown in many hotels in Nairobi and the coast.

MEDICAL CARE

Vaccinations. Check with your doctor or travel clinic well in advance, as some injections need to be taken several weeks apart. In general, your polio and tetanus boosters should be up to date, and you will need vaccinations against typhoid and hepatitis A. An inoculation against yellow fever is compulsory – you may be asked to produce a certificate at the airport proving that you have had this jab, and if you are unable to do so, you will be vaccinated on the spot.

Health precautions. You can safely swim in the sea, but avoid swimming, bathing in or drinking from lakes (especially Lake Victoria), rivers or open natural reservoirs because of the risk of bilharzia, parasites, typhoid or dysentery bacilli. All swimming pools are safe and usually well cared for. *See also Water, page 127.*

Visitors heading for the coast are advised to take all things in moderation at the start. There is a clinical condition known as 'heat exhaustion', which is generally brought about by an excess of eating or drinking, sunbathing or exercising, not just by temperature. Although sunstroke is rare on the coast, sunburn is very common since the sun is hotter and more direct near the equator.

AIDS is a serious problem in Africa. A recent report by the London School of Hygiene and Tropical Medicine claimed that 90 percent of Nairobi prostitutes tested HIV positive. Sexually transmitted diseases are common in Kenya. The major hospitals in Nairobi and Mombasa use disposable needles and syringes, but many travellers carry a small kit of their own in case medical attention is needed in remote areas.

Malaria. This is still a problem all over the country. Nairobi is officially malaria-free, but don't run unnecessary risks; take one of the several reliable prophylactics prior to your arrival in Kenya, all the time you are in the country, and as instructed by your doctor after you return home. Recommended malaria tablets for Kenya include Malarone; advantages of this drug are that it only needs to be taken for two days prior to travel, daily while in the malarial zone and one week upon return. In the majority of cases it seems to have few side effects. It is usually very expensive, however – although sometimes available on the NHS. The alternative is Larium (also known as mefloquine); in its favour, Larium is very effective and cheaper than Malarone; however, it has long been connected with unpleasant side effects including paranoia. The course also needs to be started two and a half weeks prior to travel and continued four weeks after travel. Consult your doctor as to the most appropriate type. In mosquito areas, sleep under a mosquito net (all good hotels, lodges and camps provide them – request one if it isn't already there) and use an insect repellent, preferably one containing a high percentage of DEET.

Insurance. If your medical insurance cannot be extended to foreign countries, you may want to take out special travel insurance to cover yourself in case of accident, illness or hospitalisation.

Doctors. There are highly qualified doctors, surgeons and dentists in Nairobi and Mombasa. Doctors' surgeries open 8am–5 or 6pm. Lodges in remote game reserves have resident medical staff. If travelling independently, consider joining the Flying Doctor Service as a temporary member for a small fee: PO Box 18617, 00500 Nairobi, tel: 020-315454/602492/600090, fax: 020-344170, <www.amref.org>.

Pharmacies. Pharmacists in the major urban centres take turns to stay open late, until about 8 or 9pm; rosters are published daily in newspapers. Pharmacies at the main hospitals open 24 hours a day.

Hospitals in Nairobi:
Nairobi Hospital, Argwings Kodhek Road, tel: 020-2722160, 0722-204114 or 0733-639301.
Gertrude's Garden Children's Hospital, Muthaiga Road, tel: 020-3763474/5/6, 0722-898948 or 0733-639444.
Aga Khan Hospital, 3rd Parklands Avenue, off Limuru Road, tel: 020-3662000.
Mater Misericordiae Hospital, Dunga Road South B, tel: 531199/0722-828629/0733-641870.
M.P Shah Hospital, Shivachi Road, Parklands, tel: 020-3742763/4/5.
Hospitals in Mombasa:
Mombasa Hospital, off Mama Ngina Drive, tel: 041-2312191/2.
The Aga Khan Hospital Mombasa, Vanga Road off Nyerere Ave, tel: 041-2312953.

MONEY MATTERS

Currency. Kenya's unit of currency is the Shilling (slang: Bob), divided into 100 cents (c). It is abbreviated Sh(s) and written 1/-, 2/-, etc.

There are silver coins of 50c, 1/-, 5/-, 10/-, 20/- and 40/-. Banknotes come in denominations of Shs 50/-, 100/-, 200/-, 500/- and 1000/-.

Exchange control regulations. Visitors are particularly warned against those 'unofficial' money changers who will offer incredible deals in the street – you will be breaking the law and will usually end up with a handful of paper or forged notes. Foreign currency, including travellers' cheques, may be exchanged for cash only at a commercial bank, foreign exchange bureaux or an authorised hotel.

Banking hours. Banks in Nairobi and the major inland towns are generally open Monday to Friday from 9am until 3pm and from 9am to 11am on the first and last Saturday of the month. Banks in Mombasa and along the coast open and close half an hour earlier. Some banks at the international airports open daily 24 hours.

Credit cards and travellers' cheques. Most international credit cards are accepted in Kenya, though Visa is more widely accepted than Access or Mastercard. Travellers' cheques are readily recognised and accepted at most international hotels and tourist agencies.

OPENING HOURS

Opening hours vary slightly in Nairobi, the coast and up-country towns, but in general:
Banks: 9am to 2/3pm Monday to Friday, 9 to 11am first and last Saturday of each month, excluding national holidays.
Post offices: 8.30am to 1pm and 2 to 4.30 or 5pm Monday to Friday and 8am to noon on Saturday in main post offices.
Restaurants: Breakfast is usually served 7.30–11am, lunch 12.30–2.30pm and dinner 7/7.30pm–9/10pm. In the larger cities some

restaurants will serve until midnight and you will be able to find cafes and pizzerias that serve meals throughout the day.

Shops and museums: In larger cities, generally 8.30am–5 or 6pm or up to 8pm. Variable in smaller cities or rural areas.

P

POLICE

The police are generally friendly and helpful to tourists and are the most reliable source of any kind of information you may require. If they cannot help you, they will tell you where to obtain the information you need. Tourist Police patrol the popular beaches along the coast. In an emergency, dial 999 or contact the Tourist Help Line, tel: 020-604767/605485/0722-745645/0733-617499.

POST OFFICES

Post offices are indicated by the red and blue 'Posta' sign of the Postal Corporation of Kenya. Mail boxes are painted red. You can also buy stamps at hotels and souvenir shops selling postcards. There are post offices at the main shopping centres in Nairobi and Mombasa and the international airports and major towns. Main post offices are on Haile Selassie Avenue in Nairobi and on Digo Road in Mombasa.

PUBLIC HOLIDAYS

1 January	New Year's Day
1 May	Labour Day
1 June	Madaraka (self-rule) Day
10 October	Moi Day
20 October	Kenyatta Day
12 December	Uhuru/Jamhuri (Independence) Day
25 December	Christmas Day
26 December	Boxing Day

Movable Dates
Good Friday
Easter Monday
Idd-ul-Fitr (day of feasting at the end of Ramadan)

Islamic Festivals. Muslim communities follow the Islamic calendar which varies from the Western calendar by about 11 days each year. During Ramadan, the month of fasting, most stores and cafes in Islamic districts are closed during the day, particularly in the smaller towns. Maulidi, the prophet's birthday, is a colourful celebration on the coast, especially on Lamu.

PUBLIC TRANSPORT

Buses. City buses operate in Nairobi and Mombasa and provide a good opportunity for seeing the city centres and suburbs at low rates. Visitors are advised to avoid peak hours, when the buses will be very crowded. The best times to use the city buses are from 9.30am to noon and 2.30 to 4pm. In Nairobi the clean, civilised Kenya Bus Service, Citi Hoppa and Double M operate to and from the suburbs to the city centre at regular intervals. Fares are paid on the bus.

There are no route maps on streets or at bus stops, as these change frequently. Inter-city buses of a reasonable standard connect Nairobi with all main centres, and crowded country buses link villages to the latter. On the faster routes, you may need to reserve a seat in advance.

Matatus. These mini buses are used extensively to complement the overstretched bus services between towns. Usually crammed to overflowing, matatus have an absolutely appalling safety record, and their drivers are particularly accident-prone. Recently, several laws have been brought in regarding the number of passengers carried in each bus, the wearing of seatbelts and the introduction of speed governors to reduce accidents. Theft and hijackings in matatus is also on the rise. In short, they are to be avoided at all costs.

Trains. Passenger service on Kenya's single railway line from Mombasa to Kisumu is a railway enthusiast's dream. Trains are a bit shabby and it is advisable to carry some drinks, a suitable picnic, insect repellant, toilet paper and wet wipes. The restaurant food can be good at times. Trains leave from Nairobi to Mombasa on Monday, Wednesday and Friday and return to Nairobi on Tuesday, Thursday and Sunday. Days of departure are likely to change, so check when booking. Going at the leisurely pace of 55kph (35mph), the overnight trains are timed to leave the major stations of Mombasa, Nairobi and Kisumu about sunset and to arrive at these stations around 8 or 9am. Two consecutive nights on the train can prove tiring, however, so allow for at least one night's stopover. Thefts on all trains are common, so keep an eye on your luggage.

R

RELIGION

Christianity is the dominant religion of Kenya with adherents divided roughly equally among Roman Catholic, Protestant and Independent African faiths. There are also large communities of Muslims on the coast, up-country and smaller communities in the northeastern region, where people of Somali origin live. About one-third of the rural population still adheres to a variety of traditional religions. In the urban centres, mosques and temples of various eastern faiths are much in evidence.

Nairobi is a major centre of the Independent African Church Movement. Every Sunday hundreds of groups gather on street corners, at bus stops, in parks and public halls for worship. Others march up and down the streets to the rhythm of drums in colourful clothes, carrying flags, singing and preaching. Some of the groups welcome guests, but most are suspicious of newcomers.

English services of the major Nairobi Catholic and Protestant congregations are announced in the daily newspapers on Saturdays.

S

SIGHTSEEING AND SAFARI TOURS

Numerous tour operators offer excursions to points of interest in the major towns and cities, as well as to game parks and other sights. Hotel chains organise their own sightseeing tours en route from one hotel to another. Ask at the hotel reception or travel agent for a list of possible tours and firms, and always book your tour through a legitimate office. With advance planning, you can embark on a private photo safari, guided and protected by a professional safari guide whose equipment and staff may include 4-wheel-drive cars, 5-ton lorries, trackers, camp cooks and aides. The expedition can hardly be rushed, so plan on up to a week in the Kenyan bush. This is no doubt the most exciting way of seeing the country, but the cost is prohibitive. Even a privately organised group safari is expensive, and conditions are more cramped. More affordable are the numerous special-interest safaris and tours that cater for birdwatchers, cyclists, campers and other sports and adventure holiday activities.

T

TAXIS

There are a number of reputable taxi operators in Nairobi and Mombasa (Kenatco, Jatco, Jimcab). They do not have meters, so establish the fare before getting in. Kenatco taxis are recommended. They charge per kilometre, and you can consult lists of approximate distances to prominent landmarks and places of interest posted in most good hotels. London-style black cabs are not especially reliable. Always check with the hotel reception about the approximate charge for a journey before boarding the vehicle. Private taxis come under no particular control and the vehicles may not be properly insured. Charges for waiting time and extra passengers are negotiable. In addition to these, there are long-distance taxi services, which are shared by passengers who book their destination in advance. Prices are quite reasonable, and the ride relatively comfortable. These operate only between the major urban centres and do not go off the paved roads.

TELECOMMUNICATIONS

Telephones. Telkom Kenya (<www.telkom.co.ke>) provides voice data, internet and multimedia telecommunications services. Mobile cellular services are provided by Safaricom (0720/0721/0722) and Celtel (0733/0734/0735). 'Pay As You Go' scratch cards and SIM connection kits are widely and cheaply available. Hotel call charges are generally 50–100 percent higher than the norm. Calls within East Africa are cheaper from 8pm–8am and at weekends.

Pay phones. Coin phones are painted yellow and green, while card phones are blue; they can be found throughout most towns and at major post offices and are fully automated. To use a pay phone, pick up the handset and follow the digitalised instructions on the screen to make your call. Calling Cards of different denominations can be purchased from Post Offices or international call offices in major towns.

International calls. These can be made from public call offices in Nairobi and Mombasa, where you pay for your call in advance and receive a refund if you fail to connect. Person-to-person calls are twice as expensive as station-to-station calls. There are also facilities for international direct dialling. International calls are cheaper after 8pm than during the day and discounted further after midnight. International calls can now be made through VoIP (Voice over Internet Protocol) by dialling 888 (Safaricom) or 123 (Celtel) before the country code and number. Charges start from 13Ksh plus VAT per minute.

Internet and email. There are many internet cafes in Nairobi, Mombasa and major towns, including in hotels and even some lodges. The rates range but tend overall to be very reasonable.

Useful Numbers

Long-Distance Calls: 0195/0196
Local Operator Dialling Assistance: 900
Directory Enquiries: 991/992
Customer Help Line: 980

Faxes. These can usually be sent from hotels and from most main post offices, though the latter may be very busy.

TIME DIFFERENCES

The East African countries of Kenya, Uganda and Tanzania are on standard time, three hours ahead of GMT throughout the year.

TIPPING

Tipping is not mandatory, but it is not forbidden in Kenya as it is in some of the African countries. On the other hand, you sometimes feel it is impossible to get anything done without offering a 'tip'. So if you appreciate a service, tip at your discretion, but keep it moderate.

Most good hotels and restaurants include a 10 percent service on the bill, but this is an appropriate amount to add if it isn't. At railway stations and airports 10Ksh per bag is considered usual, slightly more at hotels. It is unnecessary to tip taxi drivers, as fees should be negotiated before departure. Tour drivers, however, rely on tips to make up their wages. In general around 500Ksh per passenger per day is adequate but this can be adjusted for the quality of the service given.

TOILETS

Toilets (*choo*, pronounced 'cho') are almost always indicated in English, accompanied by the standard male and female symbols. *Wanawake* (Ladies) and *Wanaume* (Gentlemen) appear in bold letters in public lavatories and are generally warnings that the places ought to be avoided – unless in cases of extreme emergency.

TOURIST INFORMATION OFFICES

At the local tourist office staff will recommend the best shops, car-hire firms and hotels, and advise on tours, recreation and any other subject. A wide range of guidebooks, maps and pamphlets is available.

There are **Kenya Tourism Board** (<www.magicalkenya.com>) offices at Kenya Re Towers on Ragati Road on Upper Hill, PO Box 30630, 00100 Nairobi, tel: 020-2711262, fax: 020-2719925; at Jomo Kenyatta International Airport, tel: 020-827966; and at Mombasa International Airport, tel: 041-3430155.

The **Mombasa and Coast Tourist Association** (open Mon–Fri 8am–noon and 2–4.30pm, Sat 8.30am–noon, Sun 8am–noon) is located near the tusks on Moi Avenue, PO Box 99596, 80107 Kilindini, Mombasa, tel: 041-2225428/311231, email: <mcta@ikenya.com>.

Kenya Tourist Offices Abroad

UK: c/o Hills Balfour, Colechurch House, 1 London Bridge Walk, London SE1 2SX, tel: +44 (0)20 7367 0900/0929, fax: +44 (0)20 7407 3810, email: <kenya@hillsbalfour.com>.

US: Carlson Destination Marketing Services, PO Box 59159, Minneapolis, MN 55459-8257, tel: +1 866 44 KENYA, fax: +1 763 212 2533, email: <infousa@magicalkenya.com>.

Germany/Switzerland: Travel Marketing Romberg TMR GmbH, Schwarz Bach Strasse 32, 40822 Mettmann near Dusseldorf, Germany, tel: +49 (0)2104-832919.

France: c/o Interface Tourism, 11bis rue Blanche, 75009 Paris, tel: +33 01 53 25 12 07, email: <kenya@interfacetourism.com>.

Spain: c/o Aviareps, Airline Centre Espana S.L., C/Padre Damian, 40–2E 28036, Madrid, Spain, tel: +34 91458 5587, fax: +34 91 344 1726, email: <kenyaspain@aviareps.com>.

Tourist Help Line: tel: 020-604767/605485, 0722-745645 or 0733-617499, email: <safetour@wananchi.com>. Coast contacts: 0722-745644, 041- 227 721/316498. This is a 24-hour service run seven days a week by the Kenya Tourism Federation Safety and Communications Centre at the KWS Headquarters on the Langata Road, Nairobi. It has country-wide radio communications links with the Police, Kenya Wildlife Service, the Flying Doctors and members of the tourism industry. You can also call for an update of road and weather conditions. In the event that you are involved in a security incident, please call the help line.

WATER

Other than in coastal hotels, Nairobi is in theory the only place in Kenya where the tap water is safe for drinking. But this is not recommended. Use bottled or filtered water instead for everything from drinking to brushing your teeth. Nearly all lodges and camps keep bottled water or jugs of filtered water (safe to drink) beside the bed; otherwise, it is widely available in supermarkets, petrol stations and hotels.

WEBSITES

www.discoverwatamu.com	Discover Watamu
www.divingkenya.com	Diving Kenya
www.katokenya.org	Kenya Association of Tour Operators
www.kenyamuseumsociety.org	Kenya Museum Society
www.kws.go.ke	Kenya Wildlife Service
www.laikipia.org	Laikipia Wildlife Forum
www.magicalkenya.com	Kenya Tourist Board
www.mck.or.ke	Mountain Club of Kenya
www.museums.or.ke	National Museums of Kenya
www.yellowpageskenya.com	Yellow Pages

WEIGHTS AND MEASURES

The metric system is used in Kenya.

Recommended Hotels

Kenya offers a range of accommodation to suit every pocket and preference. In between the luxury hotels, the safari lodges, luxury tented camps, basic bandas are reasonable, comfortable establishments that won't cost the earth, but may be lacking in facilities. Prices vary tremendously, even within the same accommodation at different times of the year, and a star rating is not necessarily a guide to price, nor is a price guide indicative of facilities. The ranges below are given as rough guides only and are per room for one night in peak season. Note that at most lodges the rate covers full-board accommodation.

$$$$	over US$300
$$$	US$200–300
$$	US$100–200
$	less than US$100

NAIROBI

Fairview Hotel $$ *Bishops Road, PO Box 40842, 00100 Nairobi, tel: 020-2711321, fax: 020-2721320, <www.fairviewkenya.com>*. Set in 2ha (5 acres) of beautiful gardens about 2km (1 mile) from the city centre and in the tradition of a country hotel. Amenities include pool and four restaurants. Family owned.

The Grand Regency $$–$$$ *Loita Street, Uhuru Highway, PO Box 57549, 00100 Nairobi, tel: 020-211199, fax: 020-217120, <www.grandregency.co.ke>*. Formal, luxury hotel in central Nairobi. Facilities include a heated outdoor pool, casino and ten places to eat or drink, from Harry's Bar to the Summit French restaurant.

Nairobi Serena Hotel $$$$ *Nyerere Road/Kenyatta Avenue, PO Box 46302, 00100 Nairobi, tel: 020-2822000, fax: 020-2725184, <www.serenahotels.com>*. Modern hotel set in tropical gardens. Member of Leading Hotels of the World. Excellent pool, gym, sauna and steam bath. Two restaurants including the very up-market Mandhari.

Norfolk Hotel $$$$ *PO Box 40064, 00100 Nairobi, tel: 020-250900, fax: 020-250200, <www.fairmont.com>.* Nairobi's oldest hotel, on Harry Thuku Road, is set in lovely gardens, with an aviary, swimming pool, health club, beauty salon, gourmet restaurant and the Delamere Terrace bar and restaurant. Have tea on the terrace or a gin and tonic in the bar and you'll catch a whiff of the decades when the lion, the symbol of Kenya, had a Union Jack on its tail.

Sarova Stanley $$$ *PO Box 30680, 00100 Nairobi, tel: 020-2228830, fax: 020-2229388, <www.sarovahotels.com>.* Busy, comfortable hotel with large, air-conditioned rooms, swimming pool and restaurant in the heart of town. Its main claim to fame is its Thorn Tree Café in Kimathi Street. Hunters and other travellers would leave messages pinned to the trunk of a huge acacia rising in the middle of the patio. Though hunters have been replaced by tourists, and a new tree planted in 1961 (and again in the mid-1990s), the tradition holds.

Windsor Golf & Country Club $$$$ *PO Box 45587, 00100 Nairobi, tel: 020-8562300/3565501-4, fax: 020-8560160/1, <www.windsorgolfresort.com>.* As its name would suggest, this hotel is set in parklands with beautiful countryside views – and only 15 minutes from downtown Nairobi. Elegant cottages, studio suites and double rooms. Golf club, health club, sports facilities and restaurants.

SAMBURU AND SHABA NATIONAL RESERVES

Larsen's Tented Camp $$$ *Wilderness Lodges, PO Box 42788, 00100 Nairobi, tel: 020-532329, fax: 020-650384, email: <wilderness@mituminet.com>.* Luxurious facilities and outstanding comfort in a traditional tented camp. Excellent cuisine. Great for wildlife spotting too.

Samburu Game Lodge $$ *Wilderness Lodges, PO Box 42722, 00100 Nairobi, tel: 020-532329, fax: 020-650384, <www.wildernesslodges.co.ke>.* International facilities with comfortable accommodation in cottages, rooms and suites. Entertainment areas overlook the Ewaso Nyiro River. The Crocodile Bar allows close viewing of crocodiles and other wildlife on the opposite bank.

Samburu Serena Lodge $$$ *Serena Lodges and Hotels, PO Box 48690, Nairobi, tel: 020-2710511, fax: 020-2718103, <www.serena hotels.com>.* Popular lodge by the river with covered terrace bar and swimming pool. Accommodation is in attractive traditional timber cottages. There's a leopard-baiting platform across the river from the lodge and nightly crocodile feeds. 54 rooms, 8 luxury suites.

THE CENTRAL HIGHLANDS

The Ark $$$ *Fairmont Hotels and Resorts Kenya, PO Box 58581, 00200 Nairobi, tel: 020-2216940, fax: 061-55224, <www. fairmont.com>.* Upmarket tree hotel with four game-viewing areas and a bunker. Single and double cabins, all en-suite. Guests enter along a gangplank above the trees. Sightings of elephant, rhino, waterbuck, gazelle, giant forest hog and genet cats are likely.

Il N'gwesi Lodge $$$ *c/o Let's Go Travel, PO Box 60342, 00200 Nairobi, tel: 020-4447151, fax: 020-4447270, <www.letsgosafari. com>.* An award-winning community eco-lodge, built with local materials. The Maasai hosts look after the lodge and visitors' needs. The six bandas, lounge and swimming pool afford stunning views of Kenya's Northern Frontier District.

Lewa Safari Camp $$$ *PO Box 56923, 00200 Nairobi, tel: 020-600457/605108, fax: 020-605008, <www.lewasafaricamp.com>.* Secluded camp with 12 luxury tents with twin beds and en-suite bathrooms in the 45,000-acre, privately owned Lewa Conservancy (formerly a cattle ranch). Day and night game drives are offered.

Loisaba Wilderness & Koija Star Beds $$$$ *PO Box 39806, Nairobi, tel: 020-603090/1, fax: 020-603066, <www.chelipeacock. com>.* Situated in 60,000 acres of wilderness community area, on an escarpment, with gorgeous, broad views. Offers many exciting activities including a spa. Even has Star Beds on raised platforms, allowing guests to sleep under the African sky.

Mount Kenya Safari Club $$$$ *Fairmont Hotels and Resorts Kenya, PO Box 58581, 00200 Nairobi, tel: 020-2216940, fax:*

062-31316, <www.fairmont.com>. In 1959 the late Hollywood star William Holden transformed a local hotel into an African retreat for the international jet set, with landscaped gardens, golf course, riding stables and a croquet lawn. 115 rooms. Superb food. Heated swimming pool, golf course, tennis, horseback riding, croquet lawn, aviary.

The Outspan Hotel $$ *PO Box 14815. 00800, Nairobi, tel: 020-4452095-9, fax: 020-4452102, <www.aberdaresafarihotels.com>.* The base hotel for Treetops offering good facilities and stunning views toward Mount Kenya. The bedrooms are equipped with night alarms to announce the sighting of specific animals.

Serena Mountain Lodge $$$ *Serena Hotels & Lodges, PO Box 48690, Nairobi, tel: 020-2842333/2711077, fax: 020-2718102/3, <www.serenahotels.com>.* Tree hotel with friendly staff in the heart of the rainforest on the slopes of Mount Kenya. Most rooms have balconies overlooking the waterhole, where buffalo, antelope, elephant and, sometimes, lion, leopard and rhino visit. Sykes monkeys clamber along the roof and ledges (and into your room if given the chance). At 2,195m (7,200ft) nights are chilly (hot-water bottles provided), so bring an extra layer such as a fleece. Jungle walks with excellent guides and relaxing beauty treatments available. Restaurant.

Sirimon Bandas $ and Batian Guest House $ *Kenya Wildlife Services, PO Box 40241, 00100 Nairobi, tel: 020-600800, <www. kws. go.ke>.* Located in the Mount Kenya National Park. Comfortable self-catering bandas (shared bathrooms) equipped with bedding and basic equipment.

Sweetwaters Tented Camp $$ *Serena Lodges and Hotels, PO Box 48690, 00100 Nairobi, tel: 020-2842333/2711077, fax: 020-2718102/3, <www. serenahotels.com>.* Formerly the private game reserve of Adnan Kashoggi. Accommodation is in luxury tents that ring one side of the waterhole, allowing you to be out in the open air with the animals, but protected by an electric fence. There are 25 twin tents, all en-suite with hot water, electricity and flushing toilets. Other attractions include a pool, horseback and camel rides, a rhino and chimp sanctuary, night game drives and nature walks.

Treetops $$–$$$ *PO Box 14815. 00800, Nairobi, tel: 020-445 2095–9, fax: 020-4452102, <www.aberdaresafarihotels.com>.* The original tree hotel. Bedrooms have night alarms to announce the arrival of animals at the waterhole at night. Sightings of elephant, rhino, waterbuck, gazelle, giant forest hog and genet cats are typical.

THE GREAT RIFT VALLEY

Island Camp $$$ *c/o Let's Go Travel, PO Box 60342, Nairobi, tel: 020-4447151/4441705, fax: 020-4447270, <www.letsgosafari. com>.* The luxury tented Island Camp benefits from a fabulous setting on Olkokwa Island on Lake Baringo. Attractions include a pool plus all kinds of watersports and nature and bird walks.

Lake Baringo Club $–$$ *Kenya Hotels Ltd, PO Box 1686, 00600 Nairobi, tel: 020-4450712/738, fax: 020-4450735, email: <reservations@kenyahotelsltd.com>.* This is the only lodge on the shore of Lake Baringo. Attractions include bird-watching with resident ornithologist, boat trips and a swimming pool.

Lake Bogoria Spa Resort $$ *PO Box 208, Menengai West, tel: 051-2216441/2351, fax: 051-2216867, <www.mericagrouphotels. com>.* Comfortable hotel with 4 cottages, 5 minutes' drive from the reserve. Two pools, one of which is heated from a natural spring.

Lake Naivasha Country Club $$$ *Kenya Hotels Ltd., PO Box 1686, 00600 Nairobi, tel: 020-4450712/738, fax: 020-4450735, email: <reservations@kenyahotelsltd.com>.* Splendid hotel, with beautiful gardens and gorgeous views towards the lake.

Lake Nakuru Lodge $$$ *PO Box 561, 20100 Nakuru, tel: 051-850228/518, fax: 020-230962, <www.lakenakurulodge.com>.* Romantically designed rooms in an old stone farmhouse and adjacent buildings. Glorious views of the National Park. Pool and restaurant.

Sarova Lion Hill Lodge $$$ *PO Box 7094 Nakuru, tel: 037-850235, fax: 037-85212, <www.sarovahotels.com>.* Lovely views of Lake Nakuru, delicious food and massage parlour. 67 chalets.

WESTERN KENYA

Mfangano Island Camp $$$$ *Governors' Camp Kenya, PO Box 48217, 00100 Nairobi, tel: 020-2734000/1/5, fax: 020-2734023/4, <www.governorscamp.com>.* Small exclusive camp, accessible by light aircraft and speedboat, set in natural tropical gardens in a secluded bay near Lake Victoria. Just six rooms, which are in traditional Luo tribal style with mud walls and thatched roofs.

Rondo Retreat $$ *PO Box 2153, 50100 Kakamega, tel: 056-30268, fax: 056-31057, <www.rondoretreat.com>.* A tranquil retreat centre in the Kakamega Rain Forest. Good food and accommodation. Wonderful walks and views – great for avid birdwatchers.

Tea Hotel Kericho $$ *Box 75, 20200 Kericho, tel: 052-30004/5, email: <teahotel@africaonline.co.ke>.* Former Brooke Bond clubhouse with original 1950s' furnishings, pool and gardens. Guided tours of tea estate and processing factory are possible with advance notice.

Udos Bandas – Kakamega Forest $ and Kapkuro Bandas, Mount Elgon National Park $ *Kenya Wildlife Services, PO Box 40241, 00100 Nairobi, tel: 020-600800, <www.kws.go.ke>.* Comfortable self-catering bandas with bedding and basic equipment right in the forest.

MAASAI MARA NATIONAL RESERVE

Governors' Camps $$$$ *PO Box 48217, Nairobi, tel: 020-2734000/115, fax: 020-2734023/4, <www.governorscamp.com>.* Four superb old-style tented camps. All tents are the height of luxury and have en-suite bathrooms with constant hot and cold running water and flushing toilets. Governors' Camp featured in the BBC's *Big Cat Diaries*; for more intimacy, try the Little Governors' Camp.

Keekorok Lodge $$ *Wilderness Lodges, PO Box 42788, 00100 Nairobi, tel: 020-532329, fax: 020-650384, email: <www.wilderness lodges.co.ke>.* This is the oldest lodge in the Maasai Mara, set right in the centre of the park. Luxury accommodation in bungalows and chalets. There's a waterhole, for up-close game viewing.

Mara Serena Safari Lodge $$$ *Serena Hotels & Lodges, PO Box 48690, Nairobi, tel: 020-2842333/2711077, fax: 020-2718102/3, <www.serenahotels.com>*. Built in the style of a Maasai Manyatta the Mara Serena blends in well with the landscape. All amenities including a restaurant, pool and early morning hot-air ballooning. Rooms are very comfortable and offer spectacular views of the Maasai Mara.

Porini Lion Camp $$$ *Gamewatchers Safaris, PO Box 388 Village Market-00621, Nairobi, tel: 020-7123129, fax: 020-7120 864, <www.porini.com>*. A good choice for those looking for an eco-safari *(see also Amboseli Porini Camp, below)*, Porini Lion Camp is located in the 20,000-acre Olare Orok Conservancy bordering the Maasai Mara Game Reserve, on the banks of the Ntiakatiak River. There are 10 luxury tents, each with private space to enjoy the bush experience. Tents have en-suite bathrooms with flush toilets and hot showers. Game drives are in 4x4 safari vehicles. The local community earns income from these safaris. Bush walks with Maasai guides.

THE SOUTHEAST

AMBOSELI NATIONAL PARK

Amboseli Porini Camp $$$ *Gamewatchers Safaris, PO Box 388 Village Market-00621, Nairobi, tel: 020-7123129, fax: 020-7120864, <www. porini.com>*. As with the Porini Lion Camp *(see above)*, Amboseli Porini is great for those wanting an eco-safari. The camp is based in the Selenkay Conservation Area, north of the Amboseli. Accommodation and game drives as above. Maximum of 18 guests.

Amboseli Serena Lodge $$$ *Serena Hotels & Lodges, PO Box 48690, Nairobi, tel: 020-2842333/2711077, fax: 020-2718102/3, <www.serenahotels.com>*. Well-reputed lodge with 96 comfortable rooms that are grouped like a Maasai village. The novel dining room has a stream running through it.

Amboseli Sopa Lodge $$ *PO Box 72630, 00200 Nairobi, tel: 020-3750183/3750235, fax: 020-3740069, <www.sopalodges.com>*. A tourist-class lodge that is pleasant and well equipped.

Ol Tukai Lodge $$ *PO Box 45403, 00100 Nairobi, tel: 020-4445514, fax: 020-4448493, email: <oltukai@manrikgroup.com>.* Upmarket lodge with good accommodation and food and great views of Kilimanjaro.

Tortilis Camp $$$ *PO Box 39806, Nairobi, tel: 020-603090/1, fax: 020-603066, <www.chelipeacock.com>.* Award-winning eco-tourism camp with 17 spacious tents, excellent food, swimming pool, game drives, guided nature walks and great views of Kilimanjaro.

TSAVO EAST NATIONAL PARK AND ENVIRONS

Galdessa $$$ *PO Box 714, 00621 Village Market, tel: 020-7121074, fax: 020-7121099, <www.galdessa.com>.* Gorgeous camp on the banks of the Galana River overlooking the Yatta Plateau. There are even two suites with their own private viewing platforms. Extras include escorted walking safaris.

Kilalinda Lodge $$$ *PO Box 6648, 00100 Nairobi, tel: 020-882598/882028, fax: 020-882868, <www.privatewilderness.com>.* Very spacious, luxury accommodation on the banks of the Tsavo River.

Ngutuni Lodge $$ *PO Box 60342, Nairobi, tel: 020-4447151/4441030, fax: 020-4447270, <www.letsgosafari.com>.* This lodge is handy for an overnight stay on the way to or from the coast. Watering hole affords good viewing opportunities. 48 bedrooms.

Voi Safari Lodge $$ *Kenya Safari Lodges, PO Box 90414, Mombasa, tel: 041-471861/5, fax: 041-472970, <www.kenya-safari.co.ke>.* Most popular lodge in Tsavo, built high on the side of a hill. Swimming pool dug into the rock, plus waterhole and photographic hide.

TSAVO WEST NATIONAL PARK AND ENVIRONS

Finch Hatton's $$$$ *PO Box 24423, 00502 Nairobi, tel: 020-53237/8, fax: 020-553245, <www.finchhattons.com>.* This camp, named after the early 20th-century hunter-adventurer Denys Finch Hatton, is the height of luxury, with decor featuring antiques, chandeliers and crystal glasses. The camp accommodates a maximum of 50 people in large safari tents with en-suite bathrooms and large deck balconies. There is also a swimming pool. Excellent game viewing nearby, including regular sightings of hippos and crocodiles. Top-notch cuisine.

Kamboyo Guest House $$ *Kenya Wildlife Services, PO Box 40241, Nairobi, tel: 600800, <www.kws.go.ke>.* Comfortable self-catering guesthouse equipped with bedding and basic equipment in Tsavo West.

Kilaguni Serena Safari $$$ *PO Box 48690, Nairobi, tel: 020-2842333/045-340000, fax: 020-2718102/3, <www.serenahotels. com>.* The first lodge built in a Kenyan National Park, Kilaguni (meaning 'young rhino') is now in the upmarket Serena chain. Has 56 five-star rooms and a balcony looking on to a waterhole.

Ngulia Safari Lodge $$$ *Kenya Safari Lodges, PO Box 90414, Mombasa, tel: 041-471861/5, fax: 041-472970, <www.kenya-safari. co.ke>.* Ngulia is a Mecca for birdwatchers and also has a swimming pool, gorgeous views, a small airstrip nearby and a waterhole. Other attractions include leopard baiting.

Voyager Safari Camp $$ *PO Box 74888, 00200 Nairobi, tel: 020-4446651/4447929, fax: 020-4446600, <www.heritage-east africa.com>.* Situated on extreme western border of Tsavo West, this is a delightful camp with good amenities.

MOMBASA AND THE COAST

Indian Ocean Beach Club $$$ *PO Box 73, 80400, Ukunda, tel: 040-3203730/3203550, fax: 040-3203557, <www.jacarandahotels. com>.* Clusters of Swahili-style cottages house over 100 tastefully decorated rooms with verandahs and en-suite bathrooms. Amenities include several restaurants and bars (many with live music), pools (one of which is 200m/655ft), watersports, tennis, volleyball and boules. Situated on the beautiful Diani Beach, South Coast.

Nyali Beach Hotel $$$ *PO Box 40075, 00100 Nairobi, tel: 020-650500/041-471567/8, <www.nyalibeach.co.ke>.* This is one of Kenya's oldest beach hotels, located just north of town and with a fine palm beach adjacent. It's worth an upgrade to one of the lovely cottages in the pretty palm-tree-dotted grounds, as some of the standard rooms are rather uninspiring. Excellent buffet dinners – often with live entertainment – and big breakfasts. Complementary afternoon tea by the main swimming pool. Amenities include an outdoor jacuzzi, watersports, tennis courts, a disco, shopping parade and beauty parlour.

Sarova Whitesands Beach Resort $$–$$$ *PO Box 90173, 80100 Mombasa, tel: 041-5485926/5487726, fax: 041-5485652, <www.sarovahotels.com>.* A large complex with 340 rooms on Bamburi Beach and with the longest seafront on the Kenyan coast. Amenities include five pools, numerous bars and restaurants and a gym. Nightly entertainment, notably a disco at Coco's beach bar and live music.

Serena Beach Hotel and Spa $$$ *North Beach, Shanzu, PO Box 90352, Mombasa, tel: 020-2842333, fax: 020-2718102/3, <www.serenahotels.com>.* One of the most impressive hotels on the Mombasa coast, the Serena is designed to resemble a 13th-century Swahili town. It has 166 air-conditioned rooms, decorated in traditional style, and three restaurants. Recreational facilities include swimming, watersports, tennis and squash. There are also on-site gift shops, hairdressers and live entertainment.

WATAMU

Hemingways $$$–$$$$ *PO Box 267, 80202 Watamu, tel: 042-32624/32276, fax: 042-32256, <www.hemingways.co.ke>.* A member of the Small Luxury Hotels of the World, the upmarket Hemingways is undoubtedly the best hotel on the coast. It offers excellent service and food, and such extras as snacks, dubbed 'bitings', served (free) at cocktail hour – smoked sail fish and spicy prawns are typical. Guests are expected to dress for dinner (ie jackets for men). The uncrowded beach with few souvenir touts is a big advantage. Deep-sea fishing and watersports are available.

Turtle Bay Beach Club $$ *PO Box 10, 80202 Watamu, tel: 042-32003/32226, fax: 042-32268, <www.turtlebay.co.ke>*. Turtle Bay is an ideal base for the Watamu Marine National Park and is great for anyone wanting all-inclusive packages (including watersports).

MALINDI

Driftwood Beach Club $$ *PO Box 63, 80200 Malindi, tel: 20155, fax: 30712, <www.driftwoodclub.com>*. This place, just 3km (1¾ miles) south of Malindi, has a nice relaxed atmosphere. 70 rooms. The restaurant specialises in seafood. Bar. Watersports.

Malindi Beach Bandas $ *Kenya Wildlife Services, PO Box 40241, Nairobi, tel: 020-600800, <www.kws.go.ke>*. Basic self-catering bandas at Casurina Point.

LAMU

Kijani House Hotel $$–$$$ *tel: 042-633235/6/7, fax: 042-633374, <www.kijani-house.com>*. Small, exclusive hotel overlooking the entrance to Shela channel. Rooms have private verandahs and en-suite bathrooms. The pool is set in tropical gardens by the sea.

Kipungani Explorer $$$ *PO Box 74888, Nairobi, tel: 020-4446651/4444582, fax: 020-4446600, <www.heritage-eastafrica.com>*. Luxurious accommodation in chalets overlooking the ocean. Personal room stewards. Classic seafood cuisine. Watersports.

New Lamu Palace Hotel $$ *PO Box 282, 80500 Lamu, tel: 042-633164/633272, fax: 042-633164, email: <palacekey@africaonline.co.ke>*. Delightful seafront hotel with a rooftop restaurant.

Peponi Hotel $$$ *PO Box 24, 80500 Lamu, tel: 042-633154/633421, fax: 042-633029, <www.peponi-lamu.com>*. Acclaimed, traditional-style hotel at Shela beach. 24 rooms, five of which are right on the beach with private verandahs. Fresh-water, free-form swimming pool, attractively set under Baobab trees and overlooking the ocean. Dhow trips and watersports. Closed May and June.

Recommended Restaurants

Wining and dining in Kenya won't cost the earth, even at the finer restaurants. You can eat well at most establishments at far less than European or American prices. The majority of restaurants fall into the moderate range, hence we have not further classified them here; a two or three-course meal for two including drinks will usually cost between 2,000 and 5,000Ksh. Outside Nairobi and the coast your choice of eating places is slim – hotels and lodges are your best bet. (For details on average prices, refer to BUDGETING FOR YOUR TRIP, page 107).

NAIROBI

Alan Bobbe's Bistro and Gardens *24 Riverside Drive, tel: 020-4446325/3001150.* Well-established French restaurant offering great food, personal service and an intimate environment. Open Monday to Saturday for lunch and dinner.

Carnivore *Langata Road, tel: 020-605933-7/602786, <www.tamarind.co.ke>.* Very popular restaurant, where zebra, giraffe, eland, crocodile and other game is spit-roasted over charcoal and carved on to hot pewter plates at your table. For the more tender-hearted there is beef and chicken too. A favourite of Kenyans and tourists alike.

China Plate *1st Floor, Chancery Building, Valley Road, tel: 020-2719194/2727627.* Open daily. Well known for its Szechwan cuisine.

The Haandi *The Mall, Westlands, tel: 020-4448294/5/6.* Popular, high-class Indian restaurant that does great food. You can watch the chefs through a glass wall. Reservations essential.

The Horseman *Karen/Langata Road, tel: 020-882033/882782.* Food at four restaurants ranges from Chinese or Italian to English. The ambience is subtly romantic and the food is reliably excellent too.

Ibis Restaurant *Norfolk Hotel, Harry Thuku Road, tel: 020-2216940.* Smart, informal dining that offers award-winning gourmet dishes is the order of the day. Beautiful surroundings. Open for lunch and dinner.

Lord Delamere Terrace *Norfolk Hotel, Harry Thuku Road, tel: 020-2216940.* Good lunches and light meals at this popular bar; the cuisine doesn't stray far from good average international fare.

The Mandhari Restaurant *Nairobi Serena Hotel, Kenyatta Avenue, tel: 020-2822000.* Open daily for lunch and dinner. Well known for excellent quality international cuisine and discreet service.

Mediterraneo Restaurant *The Junction Shopping Centre, Ngong Road, tel: 020-3878608/3873823; Woodvale Grove, Westlands, tel: 020-4447494/4450349.* Two very popular Italian restaurants serving genuine homemade pasta and eclectic Italian dishes.

Misono Japanese Restaurant *Lenana Road, Hurlingham, tel: 020-3868959/3864961.* Open six days a week for lunch and dinner. Specialises in Sashimi, Sushi and Tepanyaki.

Pampa Grill Churrascaria *1st Floor, Panari Sky Centre, Mombasa Road, tel: 020-828132/3/4.* Open all week. Traditional south-Brazilian meat roasted in churrasco style, including a sumptuous buffet of hot and cold vegetables and salads. Brazilian wines also available.

Pango Gourmet Brasserie *The Fairview Hotel, Bishop's Road, Upper Hill, tel: 020-2881330.* Open daily; dinner only on Saturday; closed Sunday and public holidays. Fine dining with a mix of traditional brasserie fare and contemporary French dishes.

The Talisman Restaurant *Ngong Road, Karen, tel: 020-883213/0733-761449, email: <talisman@swiftkenya.com>.* Open for lunch and dinner; closed on Mondays. Set in a beautiful garden with a cosy atmosphere and a fusion of Oriental and European dishes.

Tamambo *The Mall, Westlands, tel: 020-4448064/4448394/5.* Open daily. A modern African brasserie featuring flavours from around the world. Great cocktail bar.

Tamarind *National Bank Building, Harambee Avenue, tel: 020-221811/220473, <www.tamarind.co.ke>.* Seafood is a speciality at this well-known restaurant. *See page 103.*

Trattoria, Town House *Wabera/Kaunda Street, tel: 020-340855/240205.* Ristorante, pizzeria, posticceria, cafeteria and gelateria all in one. Open 8.30am–midnight.

Verandah Garden Restaurant *Utamaduni Crafts Centre, Langata South Road, tel: 020-891798.* Good gazpacho and other Continental fare at this garden restaurant. Open daily until 5.30pm.

CENTRAL HIGHLANDS

Barney's *Nanyuki Airfield, tel: 0721-908548.* Café serving home-baked meals, steaks, burgers, pasta and sandwiches.

Mount Kenya Safari Club *Fairmont Hotels, PO Box 58581, 00200 Nairobi, tel: 020-2216940/062-30000, <www.fairmont.com>.* A superb view over Mount Kenya. Do not miss the buffet lunch bonanza.

Trout Tree Restaurant *Nanyuki/Nyeri Road, Nanyuki, tel: 062-62053/4.* Simple but delicious trout. The main restaurant is delightfully set within a Mugumo tree overlooking trout breeding ponds.

MOMBASA AND THE SOUTH COAST

Charlie Claw's Island Restaurant *Wasini Island off Shimoni. tel: 0722-410599/0733-410599.* Five-course seafood lunch: fresh, whole crab steamed in ginger, barbecue fish with Swahili sauce. *See page 83.*

Forty Thieves Beach Bar and Restaurant and Ali Barbour's Cave *Diani Beach, tel: 040-3202033/0735-331002, <www.dianibeachbar.com>.* Soak up the beach atmosphere with good seafood and pizzas.

Galaxy Chinese Restaurant *Archbishop Makarios Road, Mombasa, tel: 041-2311256; Bamburi, tel: 041-5486191; Diani Beach, tel: 040-3202529.* Open daily for cuisine prepared by a Chinese chef.

Mamba Village *Nyali, opposite the Nyali Golf Club, tel: 041-475180.* Specialises in local crocodile meat; seafood and steak also served. African buffet every Sunday.

Tamarind Restaurant, Dhow and Casino *Silos Road Nyali, tel: 041-474600/1/2, <www.tamarind.co.ke>.* Very popular seafood restaurant that serves good, fresh dishes.

Mombasa By Night *Jahazi Marine Ltd., tel: 041-472213/471895, email: <reservations.manager@severin-kenya.com>.* A sunset cruise along the shore followed by food and entertainment in Fort Jesus.

MALINDI

Baby Marrow *Vasco da Gama Road, tel: 0733-542584/801238.* Open-air restaurant serving good Italian cuisine.

La Malindina *Ngowe Street off Lamu Road, tel: 042-20045/ 31449.* Serves six or seven courses of fine Italian seafood.

Old Man and the Sea Restaurant *Vasco Da Gama Road, tel: 042-31106.* A small, popular seafood restaurant.

LAMU

Bush Gardens *On the waterfront.* Known for its seafood and kebabs, but stop in for breakfast and try the delicious mango pancakes.

Hapa Hapa *On the waterfront.* Great seafood.

Petley's Inn *On the waterfront, centre of town.* Best known for its popular rooftop bar but also serves good food.

Whispers Coffee Shop *next to Gallery Baraka and Air Kenya, tel: 042-633399/73.* Serves steak, chicken, pizza, pasta, coffee and juices.

Yogurt Inn *Harambee Avenue, southern end of town.* Set in a shady garden, this place serves excellent curries. Good vegetarian food.

INDEX

Berlitz pocket guide

Kenya

Third Edition 2008

Written by Donna Dailey
Updated by Suzie Sardelli
Edited by Clare Peel
Series Editor: Tony Halliday

Photography credits
Apa/Berlitz 6, 21, 32, 34, 37, 42, 55, 74, 77, 89,
90, 96; Mohamed Amin & Duncan Willets 43,
46; Karl Amman 30; Bodo Bondzio 1, 73; Donna
Dailey 9, 58, 88; Mary Evans Picture Library 15,
16; Glyn Genin 11, 15, 22, 27, 28, 29, 33, 48, 75,
102; David Keith Jones/Images of Africa 13, 24,
39, 56/7, 95, 98; Lawrence Lawry 8, 22, 51, 61,
62, 64, 69, 70, 76, 78, 84, 87; Dave Penman/Rex
Features 19, 98; Polyglott 50, 67; Topfoto 48

Cover picture: Art Wolfe/Getty Images

Printed in Singapore by Insight Print
Services (Pte) Ltd, 38 Joo Koon Road,
Singapore 628990. Tel: (65) 6865-1600.
Fax: (65) 6861-6438

Berlitz Trademark Reg. U.S. Patent Office
and other countries. Marca Registrada

Every effort has been made to provide
accurate information in this publication,
but changes are inevitable. The publisher
cannot be responsible for any resulting
loss, inconvenience or injury.

Contact us

At Berlitz we strive to keep our guides as
accurate and up to date as possible, but if you
find anything that has changed, or if you have
any suggestions on ways to improve this guide,
then we would be delighted to hear from you.

Berlitz Publishing, PO Box 7910,
London SE1 1WE, England.
fax: (44) 20 7403 0290
email: berlitz@apaguide.co.uk
www.berlitzpublishing.com